SUPERLEARNING 3000
Learning Made Simple

SUPERLEARNING 3000
Learning Made Simple

By

Emily Diane Gunter

Illustrated by

Kadir Nelson

Published and Distributed by: Urgent Press Publications
P. O. Box 013047, Miami, FL 33101* (305) 576-3084
First Printing, 1993
10 9 8 7 6 5
ISBN 0-9767149-3-0

Library of Congress Catalog Number 93-93-90445
Printing by Createspace   **Soft cover** **$19.95**

Dedications

I thank the Spirit, Will, Heart,

Body of My Creator for these words

that has come through me

I Thank My Newest Teachers,

My Grandchildren

Kier, Ali, Kale'a, Zane, Aya, Saliha,

Namiya, Amel, Craig, Jabril, Rashad

And

All Children Who Cross My Path

"It is my mission to bring peace to the world through

the personal empowerment and spiritual

development of all youths in Truth, Simplicity and Love."

-Emily Diane Gunter 1993

From the Original Acknowledgments - 1993

In my search for knowledge and peace of mind, I have met many authors, mentors and teachers. Their ideas have influenced many of the concepts in this book. My children, Saliha Nelson, Kadir Nelson, Amin Nelson and Shedia Nelson have taught me the most. With all my heart I want to thank my children for their unending love, guidance and encouragement to share my system of teaching and learning with the world.

I want to thank my friends, Linda Harshberger and Ruth Hall for their fine editing and assistance in putting the book into its form. I want to thank all the students of my math class at Grossmont College for their suggestions, recommendations and openness to learn math through this method and for enjoying my Superlearning 2000 teaching style.

Last but not least, I thank my parents, Fay Gaffney Gunter (1898-1972) and Verlee Gunter for their foresight to train their children to have no limits through the creative ability of their mind. My Father was a mathematician, scientist, businessman and researcher who taught his children the powers of the mind using the ancient mystery systems of Egypt and mental telepathy. My Mother taught us the religion of the Heart of Christ Consciousness and Compassion. These seeds of knowledge are now this book. I give special blessings to Jamilah Sabir-Calloway, Dr. T. L. AbuBakr Corbin, Jaime Jones, Teresa Garza and Madafo for their care during the re-editing of this book.

Note of thanks to my son, Illustrator, Kadir Nelson

My son, Kadir Nelson, is an award-winning American artist whose works have been exhibited in major national and international publications, institutions, art galleries, and museums. Kadir earned a Bachelor's degree from Pratt Institute in Brooklyn, New York and has since created paintings for a host of distinguished clients including Sports Illustrated, The Coca-Cola Company,

The United States Postal Service, Major League Baseball, and Dreamworks SKG where he worked as a visual development artist creating concept artwork for feature films, *Amistad*, and *Spirit: Stallion of the Cimarron*. Many of Kadir's paintings are in the collections of notable institutions and public collections including the U.S. House of Representatives and the National Baseball Hall of Fame, as well as in the private collections of actors, professional athletes, and musicians. Kadir has also gained acclaim for the artwork he has contributed to several NYT Best-selling picture books including his authorial debut, *WE ARE THE SHIP: The Story of Negro League Baseball, winner of the Coretta Scott King and Robert F. Sibert Awards, and was* published by Disney/Hyperion in the spring of 2008.

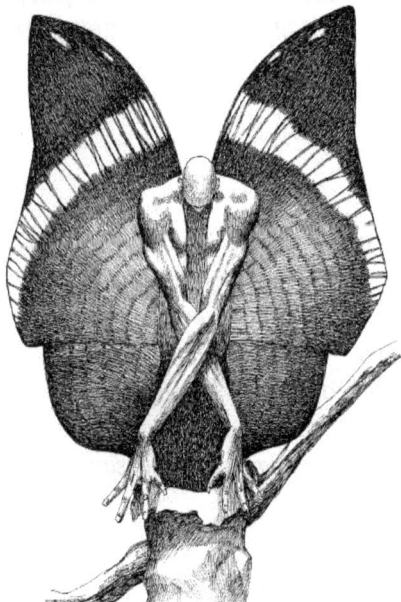

Kadir's artwork is featured on the album cover of the late pop singer icon Michael Jackson's first posthumous release entitled, *MICHAEL*. Currently (2012), Kadir is touring with his book, *Heart and Soul: The Story of America and African Americans.*

A selected list of exhibition venues includes the New York Society of Illustrators Art Gallery, the Akron Art Museum in Akron Ohio, Fort Wayne Art Museum, The Museum of African American History in Detroit, The Smithsonian Anacostia Museum Washington DC, Miami Dade College Freedom Tower Gallery, the Studio

Museum in Harlem, New York, The Bristol Museum in England, The Citizen's Gallery of Yokohama, Japan and the Center for Culture of Tijuana, Mexico. 2009 his sketch book of President Barack Obama was published. He has painted six postage stamps. He painted the Michael Jackson album cover 2010. Although Kadir works in a variety of styles, he always retains a sense of identity and focus in his work. Kadir's works are instantly recognizable by the emotion and strength of his varied subject matter. "My focus is to create images of people who demonstrate a sense of hope and nobility. I want to show the strength and integrity of the human being and the human spirit." That is exactly the feeling one walks away with after viewing one of Kadir Nelson's paintings—a feeling that runs all the way down to your DNA. **I am honored to collaborate with my son, Kadir, again for the purpose of getting this message of learning empowerment to the children of the world.** ❧

Introduction

Since my first publication in 1993 the tools of this technology have evolved. These tools give us the opportunity to acquire knowledge by linking the heart space and the mind. Listening with your heart space gives you the opportunity to live your truth and learn through your purpose in life. Breathing deeply with the use of relaxing music helps you to take in more knowledge and assimilate that information into your life.

Special Note: I was introduced to "The Healing Code" (authors: Alex Loyd and Ben Johnson) by my son, Kadir Nelson on March 1, 2013. I believe this book will help you heal the fear and anxiety you may have about learning. I suggest you practice the techniques in "The Healing Code as you read this book. Many Blessings of Peace, Muti Emily

Table of Contents

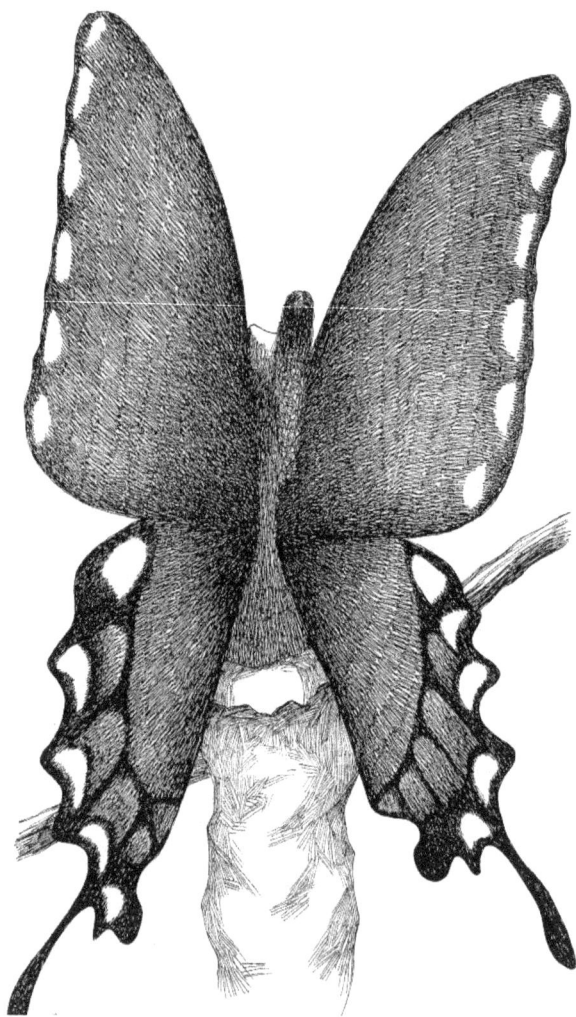

X

Preface

My adventures through the mind started as a child while playing mental telepathy games with my six brothers and sisters facilitated by my father. Then there was the fun, exciting, interactive teaching process I used for my math students at American University. The next adventure was during the birth of my first child, which I experienced with no drugs and no pain due to a conscious breathing process that I learned from Dr. Dick Reed's book, *Childbirth Without Fear*. My curiosity heightened on what the mind could do. Then I met Judy Cullins of Skill Unlimited, who taught me the foundation of the super learning technologies from the suggestopedia theories of Georgi Lozanov with sleep incubation, improved eating habits and gentle, relaxing 60 beats per minute music.

My dear friend Claudia Thompson asked me to teach mathematics at Grossmont College. Upon accepting a position to teach pre-calculus as an adjunct faculty member, I wrote my first lesson plan on *Supermath 2000: How to Learn Math Without Fear*. My students let me know that they used my process for learning for every class not just math. Therefore, my first lesson plan evolved into *Superlearning 2000: New Technologies of Self-Empowerment*.

Thanks to my daughter Saliha, I traveled to Egypt during her junior year abroad as an international student from Northwestern University to the American University of Cairo. During my visit, Dr. Muhammad Hamza, a world-renowned pediatrician, helped me crystallize the concept of linking the heart and mind for learning. He helped me to edit the manuscript by clarifying the usage of the mind versus the brain throughout this book. Rande Harvey and Jamil Garret, students at the American University of Cairo, presented me with the Kyballion. They thought I had read these ancient writings in order to write my book. I had not. This is when I knew that what I was teaching was time-honored truths. During my pilgrimage in the Himalayan Mountains of Tibet, I wrote the foundation of my book, Rites *Of Passage to Enlightenment: Living with Compassion.* The combination of *Superlearning 2000 and Rites of Passage to Enlightenment* became the Teachers' Manual complete with lesson plans and the Youth Workbook for the *Rites of Passage Youth Empowerment Curriculum.* It is a summary of all my mathematics, engineering, reading, lifelong work, books and world travels. It is my prayer that this book is a vessel, a tool of empowerment for all people who want to learn with this technology.

It is my joy to reprint the original Superlearning 2000 with edited upgrades, with the original art work of <u>my son, Kadir Nelson</u> and the 2 original covers of the first two editions. Thank you Kadir for my new cover and the enhanced title of Superlearning 3000!!

The message of this book will help our children to get to the 3rd Millennium in PEACE!! ENJOY Your Journey into a Life of Learning!!   ৩৽৻

©1993 Kadir Nelson

I

What is Superlearning 3000?

"This is a book on how to learn for life!" David Brown

From the classroom to the boardroom, young or old, rich or poor, Superlearning 3000 technology helps to prepare you for an exciting, entertaining and informative learning experience.

This book is written upon my belief that all people can learn. The Superlearning 3000 system of learning strengthens the mind, calms the emotions and enhances the thought process, which leads to a balanced learning experience.

The students designated as "at-risk" can be motivated to want to learn again, because this system empowers minds that were once discouraged. You

1

can learn effortlessly with enhanced reasoning and verbal expression, because you can learn without fear.

Superlearning 3000 is a conscious breathing method with a step-by-step approach to learning. It is a beginner's guide to more efficient use of your mind. It is an open, interesting way of thinking, which will empower you to be who you want to be, learn what you want to learn, and do what you want to do with your life. This system of learning and thinking helps you to work progressively toward a solution. This systematic approach to learning and problem solving works for all.

This accelerated learning technology includes:

- Building self esteem
- Visual goal setting
- Conscious breathing to your relaxed heart space
- Breathing to long term memory
- Pre-Reading→Speed-Seeing→Speed-Reading
- Mind mapping- Note-taking
- Sleep incubation studying
- Test taking without fear with relaxed recall
- Thought producing healthy snack breaks
- 60 beat per minute music.

This learning system produces powerful immediate results, which are predictable, repeatable, and objectively verifiable. Superlearning 3000 is being used from the elementary level to college level as prerequisite reading for all students as well as for corporate staff development.

For the purpose of clarification, this is not a scientific or technical book. This is written for students, parents, teachers, executives, trainers and educators of all levels. This is a form of learning without fear, with explanations of why and how it works.

This learning system uses the terminology of **relaxed mind** also known as the "right brain", is creative and peaceful, and **reasoning mind** to know as "the left brain" which is analytical, logical and moves the body.

The emergency response system, also known as the "fight or flight" response, represents the part of your mind, which responds to life situations, danger, panic, challenges, problems, crisis, and conflict. Whole mind represents the use of the relaxed and reasoning mind's balanced response in your relaxed heart space that is fully integrated for total mind-body coordination. I caution you to pay close attention to "how to learn," not how the brain physically works. That is for the research by scientists.

It is my belief that this book can give each lifelong learner and teacher the opportunity to know *HOW WE CAN EDUCATE OUR YOUTH TODAY*. Each of us can start the education process ourselves using the information in this book.

Using this book teachers and parents can guide their children to relax and learn without fear, which can help their children to achieve in school.

Teachers can renew their passion and excitement for teaching again and believe that all students can learn, stay in school and graduate.

Once our children increase their self-esteem, choose their purpose in life, use their special talents, geniuses and have a passion for their life of learning, they want to stay in school.

All students can learn. We can believe in them and they can believe in themselves. The skills presented can revive their passion for learning.

Teaching the students how to live through their heart space instead of behind the wall of fear, they can overcome BLAME, DOUBT and ANGER, and our schools can be safer to attend. Teachers, can change their classroom environment to an exciting place to learn with the help of the skills presented in this book. Congratulations! It is going to be fun and exciting to teach again and watch your students grow!

Students, parents, and teachers…we are all in this together. The children are our future! We can start now, TODAY, to prepare for our future. The children's success is our success.

In an ideal learning environment, our youth need to be loved, valued, understood and honored for their individual talents and geniuses. Teachers love the youth and their work with the youth. The youth are encouraged to love themselves, their talents, their genius and their work unconditionally. Teachers seek to know each youth's genius and teach specifically to that youth's genius and/or learning style. Every youth has been born with a special talent. All youth are wonderful beings who deserve compassionate assistance in removing all blocks that may be in their way of expressing their true natural gifts. Children are the foundation of our future; they are to be encouraged to start using their imagination and their dreams for our future.

‍ඉ‍ෙ‍

2
Nine Empowering Thoughts
Of a Winner

What do values; self-esteem and self-empowerment have to do with learning?
Everything!!

During the process of learning, you need to trust your mind to communicate your wisdom to you. If you are not compassionate to yourself, love yourself and believe in your own creative talents; you will never be able to hear your right answers during

7

tests. If you do not trust yourself due to your harsh judgments that you have about yourself, you will not trust in yourself enough to listen to your own internal guidance coming **through** you from your inspired self. Let's explore where you are and how you can recover those lost parts of your wisdom. You can learn to relax and learn in peace.

To achieve learning and subsequent test taking, you must trust your mind to give you the correct answer. If you do not value yourself and empower yourself for the answers or directions, you can never hear the right answer. If you do not trust yourself due to low self-esteem, you will not believe in your ability to remember how to access your knowledge.

Have you ever heard the right answer in your mind, but talked yourself out of it? Many times, you have written down the correct answer, only to go back and erase it. Why?? You changed your answers out of fear. Your reaction causes doubt, then fear. There is only one time that you can change your answers, which is when you have relaxed and retrieved more information. Never change an answer out of FEAR. Let's learn a new proactive process through empowerment, not reaction out of fear.

Learning is an attitude. If you have a good attitude towards learning, you will be more apt to do well. If you have a bad attitude toward learning, you will have difficulties in learning. Because you will constantly feel that you are not capable of learning or remembering anything, you will constantly talk yourself out of the right answer or action. I will now share with you the nine self-empowering thoughts of an achiever.

I have used this since I was an adjunct Math Instructor at American University in 1970. It is my desire that these nine self-esteem building thoughts will empower your life of learning; as much as they have empowered my life and the students that I have served.

It is important to empower yourself to accept the fact that you are the molder of your character and the master of your destiny. You can actually decide how you want to live your life. What kind of job do you want to have? How much and what you want to learn? You can visually set goals in your mind and accomplish these goals. You can have a vision for your life. This vision can become real. What must you do to make this vision become real?

Breathe!! Relax!! Dare to Dream!
Dare to Allow Your Dreams Come True!
Choose to Learn! Choose to Win!

We must empower ourselves with inspiring thoughts about ourselves so that we can be successful. These nine empowering thoughts will lead you to greater self-esteem and self-empowerment. Let us start at this point; by sitting up straight, shoulders back, taking six long deep breaths through your nose and smiling. That feels better now, doesn't it?

NINE EMPOWERING THOUGHTS

1. Choose NOW to have the life of your dreams and be able to learn anything.
YOU MUST CHOOSE, NOW.

If you don't choose, other circumstances and outside influences will choose for you. **Indecision and lack of major purpose is the biggest thief of your time**. Take several long deep breaths through your nose and imagine where you would like to be in five years.

- What is your job like?
- What is your home like?
- How do you feel emotionally?
- Is your family-life comfortable?
- Do you get to socialize with friends?
- Are you doing things you like every day?
- Are you serving others by volunteering your time?
- Do you feel your life has a purpose?
- Are you in school or back in school pursuing the career of your choice?
- Are you living up to your personal high values?
- Are you obtaining the personal growth that you desire?
- How is your physical health?
- Are you taking quiet time for yourself?
- Are you satisfied with your life?

Close your eyes and breathe deeply to imagine your life the way you want it to be. Open your eyes and write down what you felt and you saw in your mind's eye. *A wish is only a wish until you write it down*. Creative visualization is a visual goal setting technique.

Now that you have begun to choose your life proactively, you have a reason and a purpose to learn!

Everything you read, hear and experience in class from this moment on, will apply in some way to your life and career. So let us learn to take an "A" in our studies whether it is in the classroom or in the boardroom.

2. Have a Passion for Life and for Learning.

Choose to risk living fully each day of your life. Wake up each morning with the passion and excitement for life. Throughout the rest of this book, we will focus on, how to have a passion for life using the Superlearning 3000 techniques. You have another opportunity, another day to continue to work towards your dreams and aspirations. You see around you the miracle of life through your mind. You see your inspired mind guiding you closer to the goals that you have just visualized. You are now proactive in your pursuit of your goals. By being proactive, I mean you are not sitting around waiting for something to happen. You make minute-by-minute choices to move toward your goals. You are starting your success. Dare to dream. Dare to allow your dreams come true. Dare to learn anything you want.

3. Be an Inspirational Thinker.

For the next 30 days, monitor your language and your thoughts. You have thousands of thoughts every day. Every time an uninspired thought comes into your mind, take a deep breath through your nose. Say, "Cancel! Cancel!! Breathe deeply twice and then say **"you can go quietly now!!"** This stops the emotions from reacting and moving you into a space of fear. Now, hear and act on the opposite inspired thought instead. Continue to do this conscious breathing until you hear a more empowering thought and feel calmer. *One long breath in to the count of seven and a long deep breath out to the count of 10 equals 17 seconds of silence. This silence allows your deep inner wisdom to come forth.* You may be breathing deeply a lot for the next 30 days.

Practice having no judgment against any of your uninspired thoughts. Just breathe and let the uninspired thoughts fade away. When you hear yourself saying uninspired things aloud or in your mind about yourself or another person, take a deep breath and replace it's opposite. If you hear yourself saying to yourself, **"I can't, I can't!"** stop and take a deep breath and say, **"Yes, I can!"** For the next 30 days be determined to release yourself of uninspired, stressing, disturbing and worrying thoughts. You will be creating the habit of being an inspirational thinker.

The mind can only hold one thought at a time, inspired or uninspired. **Choose now** to let that thought be inspiring. When you choose to have inspiring thoughts, you choose to have a great attitude. When you choose to have a great attitude you choose to have wonderful events drawn to you as you move nearer to your goals and desires. Likewise, when you choose to have uninspiring thoughts, you are choosing a doubtful attitude, consequently, choosing destructive events to be drawn to you and pushing you away from your desires and goals.

You are the sum total of your experiences. It is your nature to be inspired first. Using simple mathematics, wonderful experiences add up to an empowered life. Fearful experiences add up to a miserable life. A life full of half positive (+) and half negative (-) experiences leaves you with (0), stuck in a rut, going nowhere. However, if you acknowledge and learn from your fearful experiences, you can move forward in an empowered direction.

You are an equation. Every equation is energy. Energy is Love. The sum total of all equations makes up our planet. **Each one of us is an important part of the equation of life**. Choose now to live in harmony with the wonderful energy of our planet. When you do, you choose to relax and learn.

4. Believe in Yourself. Believe You Can Learn.

You must believe in yourself. If you do not believe in yourself, no one else will believe in you either, and "Why should they?" When you set your goals, you must believe with a deep passion that you have it within yourself to accomplish what you have set out to achieve. Let no one tell you that you cannot achieve your goal, no matter how great or small. **You can achieve anything you want as long as you are willing to take the path to get to it, in an inspired way.**

The only person who can tell you "**no**" is yourself. When someone says "**no**" to you, only you can turn around and say, **"Yes, I can! I am**

enough!" Love and respect yourself. Be true to yourself! Our self-concept rules our lives. Our self-concept can be a wonderful encourager or a tyrannical dictator stopping our every effort. Believe in yourself!

When you believe in yourself, others will believe in you, too! Others will hear what you have to say and support you. You cannot waiver on this, because others will not take you seriously. Say, "Yes, I can!" and believe it. Say, "I can achieve," "I can learn," "I can tell myself the correct answer." Say "YES" to yourself and life events. Then life events say "YES" back to you like a circle.

5. Anticipate Problems. Have a Strategy!

There is disruptive energy that we must deal with. Know this fact. Anticipate problems. Meet these problems with decisiveness. Be proactive in dealing with problems. Be proactive in planning, not reactive. *Whenever there is a crisis, know there is also an opportunity.* In the same frightening experience, there is an adventure. The strategy for dealing with crisis and disruptive events is simple. Take several deep breaths through your nose and switch your mind from its emergency mode, into the relaxation mode, and give yourself the ability to **see the opportunity in the crisis.** Using this strategy, you will now accept what may appear to be a setback, as an opportunity for a step forward.

Let the chips fall where they may. It is what you do with these chips that make the difference in how they impact your life. Keep your eye on your vision and your goals. When you take your eye off your vision, you will see the problems. See, feel and assess the problem quickly. Dwelling on these problems may send your mind into fear. Hence, keep your eye on your vision and believe that you can live this vision as a reality in your life.

6. Have High Values

Your basic beliefs are the foundation which you set your standards and values for your life. If you are not sure of what your personal values are, keep reading. I have more on choosing your personal values. When times get rough, you must go back to your foundation.

Choose now to live your high values.

Choose now to have a stern regard for duty.

Choose now to have high regard for human life.

Choose now to have a sense of nobility.

Choose now to have courage.

Choose now to live in truth.

Choose now to live with justice.

Choose now to live with clarity.

Choose now to live with simplicity.

Choose now to live the life of your dreams.

Choose now to live with a loving heart.

Choose now to be responsible for your actions.

Choose now to be responsible for your life.

Choose to be worthy.

Choose to enjoy your work.

Choose to have patience.

Choose to practice your skills and talents/geniuses.

Choose to be of good service to others.

Choose now to breathe deeply and relax so your inspired thoughts can flow. Let your highest values guide you. Congratulations on your choices!

7. Have Bonding Power.

I am because we are, we are because I am.
--African Proverb

We are our brothers' and sisters' keeper, if only to be kind to them and respect them as fellow human beings. We are not alone on this planet. We are all tied together in one gigantic mathematical equation. We are the sum total of humankind: our mothers, fathers, sisters, brothers, teachers, mentors, bosses, peers, co-workers, the people who serve us in the stores, service our cars, farm our food, make our clothes and on and on. This list is endless for we are all tied together in some way to make each other's lives easier, better and richer.

Choose to bond with those around you. We are all submerged in the same air. We breathe in each other's essence every day. I am you and you are me! It has been said that there are only six degrees of separation between each of us. This means that there are 6 people away from the very person you want to meet and have a business or personal relationship with. *You never know who is in the body until you really get to know a person.*

Choose to have courtesy,
kindness and respect for all people in
Truth, Simplicity and Love.

Let's take a moment to examine the three ingredients of courtesy, kindness and respect.

"COURTESY" – This is the high value of being polite and showing considerate behavior toward another human being. This is a choice. You choose to have high values to guide your life towards others. Courteous and gracious manners will bond you to all the people who could assist you in attaining to your future.

"KINDNESS" – This is the high quality of being friendly, thoughtful and gentle to others. When you give these qualities to others, you give these qualities to yourself. The best way to show your kindness is to start with a SMILE! Your SMILE will automatically let others know that you appreciate them and their special talents, whatever that might be. Choose to bond through your smile.

"RESPECT" – Respect is the special esteem or consideration in which one holds another person. You must first respect yourself, honor your own worth and hold yourself in high esteem. When you respect others and yourself, you bond with them. The powerful words "THANK YOU", say "*I respect what you have done for me*", and bond the association.

The courteous, kind and respectful gesture of SMILING and the words THANK YOU, will bond you with all people around the world. Courtesy, kindness and respect are your best traveling companions, as you set out on your adventure to learn, to be, to have and to do anything you want in your life. **Live with mutual admiration, appreciation and cooperation for all humanity.** *HAPPY BONDING!*

8. Have Vibrant Energy.

Direct your energy with heartfelt intelligence. When you breathe deeply to relax, you have the opportunity to use endorphins that give you an abundance of energy for long periods of time. Choose to not waste your energy on unhealthy thoughts and actions. **Smile!** Send your bright smile out and watch so many others send it right back. You get energized every time a smile is returned.

To have vibrant energy is a choice! Choose to have a simple healthy mental diet while studying. It is very draining to live in fear, doubt, and anger. When you are relaxed, you draw on the inspired energy coming through you. When you are inspired you move toward **Courage** to be who you want to be, you have **Clarity** of the goals you want to accomplish, and you have **Self-Control** to live your high values in attaining your goals.

When your thoughts, feelings and emotions are aligned in peace, your actions and deeds give you vibrant energy. Each day choose to use your highest values and your deepest wisdom through your heart space in your body. Breathe deeply through your nose and relax and choose to have vibrant energy.

9. **Be a Professional Communicator.**

To be a professional communicator, **first listen.** Listening provides the opportunity to take six deep breaths to get to your heart space and see the whole situation from an objective position. This is important especially if the person speaking is being combative. By listening first you will hear their concerns and remain open to hear everything else they have to say. You want truly to understand, what they are saying.

Have the courage to verify that you heard what they said: 1) Repeat back to them what you heard, 2) allow them to correct you if you did not hear them correctly. 3) Check in with them one more time to see if there is anything else that they need to say. 4) If yes, keep going through this process until they have told you everything they need to. 5) If they start to repeat themselves, you know they have shared all they can. 6) In a respectful way, let them know you would like to share your thoughts.

Now, it is your turn to express your views on this situation. It is important that the other person fully understands your perception. It is up to you to be clear about what you need to say to be understood. You have been in your relaxed response mode where your mental perception can see the whole picture with no gaps. You can understand everyone's position and they can benefit from the results of this exchange. By listening first, are able to mentor, teach and coach to a proactive solution. This process is a win-win for everyone involved.

Ask the other party if they understand what you are saying. If they have misunderstood any portion of your part, clarify right then. Have them repeat back to you what you have said to insure that they truly heard what you meant. Now sincere and honest communication is happening.

The professional communicator inquires immediately to understand any situation, and then speaks out on the spot, with firmness, honesty and kindness. If you miss the opportunity to inquire immediately on an issue, wait until it arises again. To try to dig up old issues that are no longer current is counter-productive. Communicating in the present moment is most effective. You will increase your opportunity to learn, when you truly listen first to those instructing you.

As a professional communicator, when you listen first and breathe to your relax response system, your demeanor will be charming, respectful and courteous. The person you are communicating with will be inclined to treat you this way, also.

One last comment: Remember to ask yourself before you respond to any situation:

1. Is it true? If you are not sure, keep your comments to yourself and release attachment. It is not necessary to comment.

2. Is it necessary? If not sure, keep your comments to yourself and release attachment again.

3. Is it kind? If not, do not speak! Release attachment. All unkindness, remains in your body as dis-ease.

Choosing Your Values

Only you can choose your values. You have values that rule you on the unconscious level. Close your eyes breathe deeply and go inside of your heart space for 17 seconds and choose your life values. Below there are two sets of values. One set will help you to identify your **purpose** in life. I will call the first set, **Mission Life Values.** Your Mission Life Values reflect "**WHAT**" you want for yourself, your family, your loving relationships, your life's works, your community work, home, health and personal growth. The second set is your **Goal Life Values**. These values help you to identify "**HOW**" you will live your life to accomplish your purpose or mission in life.

Below, please read the entire list of Mission Life Values, then go back and check off seven boxes of those values that describe what you want out of life that money cannot buy. These ideals are closest to your **heart**. Make your check marks in the boxes in the left margin. Next, prioritize the seven mission values you have just chosen by writing the 1 to 7 next to the box. If "LOVE" is your top value, write "Love" on line one (**1**). Then proceed to choose the second value and write the word on line number two (**2**). Keep going until you prioritize your top seven mission life values.

KNOW YOUR TRUE LIFE VALUES
(WHAT?) MISSION LIFE VALUES   **Your Purpose Life**

❑	**ACHIEVEMENT**- Attainment of goals	1._____
❑	**ADVENTURE** - Pursuing excitement	2._____
❑	**AESTHETICS** - Appreciation of the arts	3._____
❑	**AFFLUENCE** - Wealth, ease of prosperity	4._____
❑	**COMPASSION**- Empathy toward self/others	5._____
❑	**EMPOWERMENT**-Inspiration over oneself	6._____
❑	**EQUALITY** - Justice and fairness for all	7._____
❑	**FREEDOM** - Independence in thought/life	8._____
❑	**FELLOWSHIP** -Having valued relationship	9._____
❑	**HAPPINESS** -Joy and contentment	10._____
❑	**HEALTH** - Sound body and mind	11._____
❑	**LOVE** - Intimacy, devotion, warmth	12._____
❑	**NATURE** - Respect for animals/environment	13._____
❑	**PEACE**- Freedom from violence	14._____
❑	**PLEASURE** - Entertainment and fun	15._____
❑	**POWER** – Leadership through purpose	16._____

21

❑ **RECOGNITION -** Known for your works 17._____

❑ **SELF-WORTH** - High regard for self/others 18._____

❑ **SOCIAL SERVICE** - Helping others   19._____

❑ **SPIRITUALITY** - At one with the Creator 20._____

❑ **WISDOM** - Insight and understanding   21._____

Now do the same prioritizing exercise for your Goal Life Values. After you have prioritized your top seven Goal Life Values, return to the Mission Life Values and prioritize the rest of the list, then finally, prioritize the rest of your Goal Life Values.

(HOW?) GOALS IN LIFE VALUES	Your Goals Life
❑ **ACCOUNTABILITY** - Responsible, credible	1._____
❑ **AFFECTION** - Passionate, loving, caring	2._____
❑ **AUTONOMY** - Self-reliant, self-directed	3._____
❑ **COMPETENCY** - Productivity, efficiency	4._____
❑ **COURAGE** - Brave and fearless	5._____
❑ **CREATIVITY** – Inventive, original	6._____
❑ **DISCIPLINE** - Restrained, self-controlled	7._____
❑ **DRIVE** - Industrious, goal directed	8._____
❑ **FAIRNESS**-Unbiased, impartial, honorable	9._____
❑ **FLEXIBILITY** - Adaptable, able to change	10._____
❑ **FORGIVENESS** - Understand and let go	11._____
❑ **HONESTY** - Truthful, trustworthy	12._____
❑ **HUMOR** - Light-hearted, witty, funny	13._____
❑ **KNOWLEDGE** - Intellectual, scholarly	14._____
❑ **LOYALTY** - Dedicated, devoted, steadfast	15._____
❑ **OBEDIENCE** - Compliant, yielding	16._____
❑ **ORDER** - Systematic organized	17._____
❑ **REASON** - Rational, analytical, logical	18._____
❑ **SERVICE** - Supportive, aiding, assisting	19._____
❑ **TOLERANCE** - Open, accepting, patience	20_____
❑ **WISDOM** - Insight, understanding	21._____

Your Mission Life Values describe WHAT you want to accomplish in your life. Your Goal Life Values describe HOW you choose to accomplish your purpose and mission in your lifetime. How will you live your life? How will you live your highest goal life values? So much so, that you get to be and have what you want?

Now that you have chosen your mission and goal life values, you are closer to understanding your purpose in this life. When you understand your purpose, you understand that you have a special talent to share with the world. Knowing this purpose for your life gives you a sense of passion and drive for learning everything that you can that relates to your purpose. Now you have a reason to LEARN. Everything you read and hear will apply in some way to your passion and career.

"Indecision and lack of major purpose

is the biggest thief of time"

Knowing your purpose for your life is the major key to learning. Once you know why you are on this planet and <u>the greater purpose you choose</u> to fulfill, you have a reason for wanting to learn all you can. What is the purpose for your life? You and only you can choose this purpose. If you do not know what your purpose is, how do you find out? Your purpose is directly linked to your mission and goal life values. Your purpose can be identified through your deep passion felt by your highest mission life values, of what you want out of life that money cannot buy. How do you live your life through your highest goal-life values, to be what you want to be and to get what you want to have? This choice must be made by you **now**!!!

Everyone was born with special talents and geniuses to contribute to the world in fulfilling their purpose/mission. When you choose to exercise your free will, you will have a greater opportunity to use your special talents and gifts to live that purpose.

Use your top seven Mission Life Values to describe and write your Mission Statement. "**If you have all the time, energy, money, wisdom and compassion to accomplish anything that you want to do, what would you do?**" Get yourself a journal.   Date the page. Put the title "Mission Statement" at the top of the page. Next, write your first seven Mission/Purpose Life Values at the top of the page. Go back to your list of Mission Values and record your values below: (You didn't complete it?? Can you do it now, please?)

    1.   2.   3.
    4.   5.   6.   7.

Ask yourself, "What do I want to accomplish in a year, or 5 years, or 10 years from now"? _**A wish is only a wish until you write it down**_. Your words set your destiny.   When your Mission Statement is written with deep commitment and reviewed, it becomes a contract between you and your inspired self.

Begin the statement with something like... "By the year _____, it is My Mission to...", then start to write down what you want to accomplish for your life. First, write a sentence with the 7 mission values in it, then expand your life with the full story of what you want to accomplish. Do not worry about the grammar! Just tell yourself "WHAT" you want out of life that is good, comforting and will do harm to no one. If someone must lose for you to have the life you want, think again on how it can be a win-win situation for all. How can I have the life I want without hurting someone else? Remember; **Use your seven top Mission Life Values in your initial Mission Statement**. <u>Underline</u> each value in your statement or use the synonyms of your values.

Here is an example of a Mission Statement using the Mission Life Values of:

1. Spirituality
2. Peace
3. Love
4. Social Service
5. Wisdom
6. Empowerment
7. Compassion

"By the year 2020, it is my mission to bring <u>peace</u> and <u>compassion</u> to our world through the personal <u>empowerment</u> and <u>spiritual</u> development of all humanity (<u>social service</u>) in truth (<u>wisdom</u>), simplicity and <u>love</u>."

When you finish your initial Mission Statement, expand this into pages of dreams with details about your purpose in life, family; loving relationships, education, job, career, home, transportation, personal health, personal growth, and heritage/community volunteer work. Make sure your top seven Mission Life Values are included throughout your description of each part your life dream.

Write this mission statement as if no one is going to read it. You can only share this information with those who love you unconditionally and who would never laugh at your dreams. Chances are that those who would laugh at your dreams have none of their own or are insecure about their opportunities in life (forgive them and move on). **Only if you dream can your dreams come true.** Sign and date your Mission Statement at the end. Remember, your signature is your <u>Seal</u> for your contract with your life.

When you finish your expanded Mission Statement, write your Goal Statement. **If you had all the time, energy, money, wisdom and compassion to accomplish all that you wrote in your above Mission Statement, "How would you accomplish it?"** A wish is only a wish until you write it down. Date this page. Put the title "Goal Statement" at the top. Next, write your seven top Goal Life Values at the top. Go back to your Goal Values and record your values below:

1.   2.   3.

4.   5.   6.   7.

Begin your statement with something like..."**By the year _____, my Goal is to accomplish My Mission by...**" Tell yourself **HOW** you are going to accomplish all that you affirmed in your mission statement. Make sure your top seven Goal Life Values are included in your Goal Statement and <u>underlined</u>. When you finish your initial Goal Statement, write the expanded version on **HOW** you are going to achieve each part of your dream. Be sure to use your Goal Life Values throughout this expanded description also. As you see and feel the changes in your life, record your successes in your journal. As the years go by, review your journals to feel your progress.

Here is an example of a Goal Statement using the seven top Goal Life Values of:

1.   Courage
2.   Creativity
3.   Honesty
4.   Fairness
5.   Forgiveness
6.   Humor
7.   Service

"By the year 2020, it is my goal to accomplish my mission by having the courage to speak the truth (wisdom) and stand up for the youth while using my creativity. I shall be honest, humorous and fair with those I work with. I shall forgive those who choose not honor the idea that all youth can learn."

In conclusion, choosing your purpose destiny is your path to learning. You can learn your life's purpose by getting quiet and searching your heart. Only you can answer the questions that I have asked you up to this point. Choose what level of knowledge and wisdom for which you are willing to be responsible. From what level will you act with your **true response?** Are you willing to get quiet enough to hear your inspired self? **This information comes through you.**

Your life experiences are the result of your daily thoughts. Every time you have a thought, your body manifests a small particle in your body. What does that mean? It means that your body produces a molecule in your body that relates directly to your thoughts. You are producing many molecules in your body every day. Do these molecules feel comfortable or uncomfortable? **We experience these thoughts as words, actions, emotions or feelings.** The thoughts will manifest as ease and comfort in your body or dis-ease and discomfort in your body. How is your life adding up so far? Your body talks to you. How does your body feel? Do you want to change the way you feel? Do you want to   change   your   life?

Choose   to   change   your   thoughts. Compassionate thoughts help you to change your life and learn whatever you want. You were born with special   talents   and   creative   geniuses.   Your compassionate, unconditional loving thoughts about yourself help you to recognize and to choose to use your   creative   geniuses/special   talents   in   your   life. Please, love yourself enough to relax and embrace your special talents, creative genius and enjoy the life that   you   envision   in   your   mission   and   goal statements.   You   are   what   you   give   out.

CHOOSE NOW TO LEARN AGAIN IN JOY USING   YOUR   HIGHEST   VALUES!

☙❧

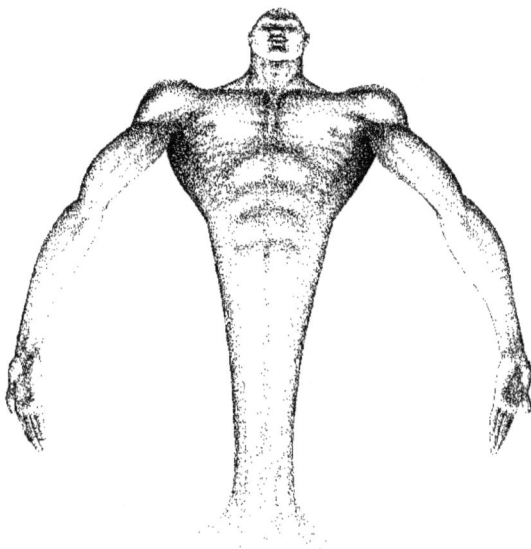

©1993 Kadir Nelson

3
Breathe in Knowledge
BREATHE TO RELAX TO LEARN

Conscious breathing is the key to the Superlearning 3000 techniques. Conscious breathing is the process of paying attention to how you are breathing. The conscious breathing will stimulate learning, assist in getting to long-term memory, unlock your brain's resources, and keep you relaxed during the learning process.

Conscious breathing is the foundation of learning. As you consciously breathe, you gain more access to the power of your mind, which houses your memory and knowledge and simultaneously equalizes your mental thought and keeps you focused. Deep relaxing breaths calm the restless reasoning mind that is eager to analyze anything, whether it has all the information or not. Conscious breathing helps you to maintain your composure during crises and frightening experiences. Breathing to stay in your relaxed heart space will give you the ability to conquer fear and despair, while learning.

What is Conscious Breathing?

Conscious breathing is the process of controlling your breathing pattern. When you take a deep breath through your nose you begin to feel more relaxed and ideas become clearer. When you lose something, it is not until you calm down and relax that your mind will tell you where to find it. The part of your mind that will tell you where to find your misplaced item is the part of the mind you are about to learn how to use more productively through deep breathing.

Conscious breathing relaxes you and places you in your relaxed mind. When you breathe slowly and deeply, your relaxed system turns on in your heart space. While you are in your emergency response system we react as if we have to fight or take flight, in other words, to defend ourselves or to flee quickly from a situation. **Learning is not a frightening experience, so there is no need to be in our emergency system.** Your emergency response system operates on adrenaline energy. Your relaxed response system in your heart space operates on endorphins; the body's natural healing agents. Sustained use of adrenaline causes stress and can eventually cause disease in your body. You don't have to die to learn. Learning is a living experience.

What does breathing really have to do with learning?

Our learning takes place in our relaxed system. **The more you are relaxed the more you learn.** You cannot be stressed and relaxed at the same time. We typically do not learn well under stress. You cannot be in fear and have courage at the same time. You cannot have doubt and be clear at the same time. Choose to be relaxed. **Choose to consciously breathe to your relaxed system, hence choose to learn.** As you breathe in, information is stored into long-term memory in your relaxed mind. You breathe to put information in your long-term memory and you breathe to take it out. You will have more retention and recall using this breathing technique.

How do you consciously breathe to get in to your relaxed mind?

How fast do you breathe now? It is important that you observe how you currently breathe. Time yourself for one minute. Count on the out breath. See how many complete breaths you take in one minute. How many times did you breathe? ....10?...20?...30?...40? Most people breathe 20 to 40 times a minute. Now that you know how fast you are breathing, it is important that you make conscious effort to slow down your breathing to about four to six breaths in a minute.

Cleansing Breath

The First breath is the cleansing breath: Breathe in through the nose to the count of 7 and breathe out to the count of 10 through

the nose or the mouth. Cough when there is no more air.

THEN Second…

Deep Conscious Breathing (six sets)

- **Breathe in through the nose to the count of seven.**
- **Hold for one brief count as you sniff in.**
- **(CAUTION! If you have high blood pressure, do not hold for one count).**
- **Breathe out through your nose or mouth to the count of seven.**

It is also important that you breathe in through your nose because the hairs in your nose are not just there to keep out dust and germs. The oxygen gets warm as it passes over the hairs in your nose. This warm oxygen going into the brain switches on your relaxed response system, therefore turning on your relaxed creative mind and your special talents. You get the same relaxed feeling when you drink a warm cup of tea or slip into a warm bath.

You hold your breath for one count to allow your blood the opportunity to gather used oxygen with waste in it and to take up more new fresh oxygen. When you blow out through your mouth to the count of ten, you release all the old oxygen full of waste, which needs to be expelled from your body. For the first few times of breathing out to the count of ten, cough after there is no more air to breathe out.. You may continue to cough involuntarily for the next few hours because the body will want to continue to cough out waste.

After your 1ˢᵗ cleansing breath continue to breathe in and out comfortably to the count of seven. Make the conscious breathing your normal breath. Six sets will get you to your relaxed heart space. The reason you count is to assist you to breathe in fully and to breathe out fully. After 30 days of practice you will not need to count anymore. This breathing pattern will become your new life enhancing habit.

Most of us only use a small portion of our lungs. It is important to fill up our lungs completely with fresh oxygen and release all old oxygen full of waste. Breathe in through the nose and watch your abdomen expand. Keep breathing in and watch the side of your ribs and upper chest and shoulders fill with life giving oxygen. Then sniff to fill your lungs completely. You have just filled up your lungs to full capacity. If you have high pressure, do not hold your breath.

Another way to release more waste out your lungs at the beginning stages of your conscious breathing is to bend over at the waist, as you breath out, until your head is as far down toward your knees as you can get (like doing a toe touch). You can also use this method while sitting on your knees and bending over while breathing out to the count of 10 until your head touches the floor in front of you. Breathe out the count of 10 as you bend over in both positions and breathe in to the count of six when you rise up. You are also massaging your abdomen as you bend over.

Here are three breathing exercises I learned from Dr. Asar Hapi. These exercises will help you to fill your lungs completely and expel the used oxygen completely. Start with five sets and then add one more set each day for 30 days.

Exercise #1

- Stand with your feet about a foot apart.
- Keep your spine straight. Head up.
- Relax your knees, and go limp.
- Let your hands hang loose next to your body.
- Breathe in to the count of seven as you raise your arms up and over your head.
- Let the backs of your hands touch
- Hold your breath for one count or sniff.
- Now lower your arms slowly back to the side of your body as you breathe out to the count of seven.

Exercise #2

- Stand with your feet apart.
- Keep your spine straight. Head straight.
- Relax your knees by bending them slightly.
- Go limp with your hands limp by your side.
- Place right hand on top of the left hand (For Females)-palms facing up.
- Place left hand on top of the right hand (For Males) palms facing up.
- Let your thumbs touch
- Raise your elbows up with palms facing up until your elbows are even with your shoulders.
- Breathe in to the count of seven as you raise your arms.
- Turn your hands over so your palms are facing down as you count to one or sniff.

- Push your hands down as you breathe out to the count of seven.

Exercise #3

- Stand with your feet apart.
- Circle your arms in front of you. (Crossing your arms in front of you)
- Raise your arms by swinging them up and crossing them in front of your body.
- Breathe in to the count of seven as you raise your arms.
- Hold for one count or sniff as you turn your palms down.
- Lower your arms back down to your side as you breathe out to the count of seven.

These breathing exercises enlarge your body's capacity to process oxygen. Conscious breathing enhances the respiratory system and the cardiovascular system. Therefore, the whole body is enhanced. Expanding the breath nourishes all the cells of the body. More oxygen strengthens the nervous system. All organs will perform more effectively, especially the brain. The brain may only be 2% of the body's weight, but it uses 20% of all oxygen consumed by the body. Breathe to give the brain the oxygen it needs to open your mind to store more knowledge.

Breathing Exercises While Sitting

During class, tests and seminars, it is not possible to stand up and do the exercises just described. There are times even while you are studying that you do not want to actually get up and exercise. The following exercise can be done at your seat or desk along with your breathing exercises.

Exercise #1

As you breathe in to the count of seven (7) and out to the count of seven (7), massage each hand thoroughly, (i.e. each finger and the palm especially the thumbs). **The nerve endings of your brain are in your thumbs. So turn that brain on!** When both hands are completely massaged, shake out the hands.

Exercise #2

As you breathe in to the count of seven (7) and out to the count of seven (7), rotate your head and neck slowly in each direction in a semi-circle. After each complete breath, change directions.

Exercise #3

As you breathe in to the count of seven, raise your shoulders up towards your ears. Then breathe out to the count of seven, and drop your shoulders.

Exercise #4

As you breathe in to the count of seven, rotate your foot at the ankle clockwise. As you breathe out to the count seven, rotate your foot at the ankle counterclockwise. Rotate each foot.

Exercise #5

As you breathe in to the count of seven (7) and out to the count of seven (7), gently massage your head starting at the temples and down around the lower jaw. This gentle massage is done with the fingertips.

Do these exercises until you have completed at least six sets of your breathing exercises. One set includes breathing in to the count of seven (7) and out to the count of seven (7). Breathe and exercise until you are relaxed. After your exercises with your cleansing breaths, continue to breathe in your relaxed posture by breathing in to the count of seven and out to the count of seven. Your counting may be slightly longer or shorter. Find your relaxed rhythm pattern.

Music to Learn By

The 60 beats per minute music help to maintain your conscious breathing pattern which will keep you in your relaxed heart space where your learning takes place. Conscious breathing to 60 beats per minute music, such as Baroque, helps to keep you in your relaxed heart space for learning.

The 60 beats per minute music are important because that is your approximate relaxed heart rate. The vibration of the music is an equation. Your body has its vibration that can be translated to an equation. Allow the vibration of the music to infuse with your vibration to help you to relax. The music helps to create a peaceful relaxed environment, prime for learning and using long term memory. The music helps to remind you to breathe and stay relaxed. When you are studying with music in the background and you begin to notice the music that is a reminder to breathe deeply. While you are in your relaxed system, you do not consciously hear the music.

When should you consciously breathe and why?

Event	Results You Will Experience
Before a test/exam	Answers come clearer

During a crisis	Crisis turns into
opportunity	
In stress	Become Relaxed
In fear	Have Courage
Angry	Become calm and in
control	
In Doubt	Become clear
Creating new ideas	Ideas flow
In class	Become interested
Uninspiring Emotions	Inspiring emotions
Public appearance	Calm, repose, in
control	
Any big moment	Calm, repose, in
control	
Moments of panic	Calm, ability to respond
Stomach distress	Calm, relaxed
Tightness of larynx	Ability to speak fluently
Poor circulation	Enhanced circulation
Fast pulse	Calm, d repose
Competitions	Total coordination
Surgery	Heal faster
All business meetings	Relaxed, clear, in
control	
All personal meetings	Relaxed, clear, in
control	

When I have extra stressful events about to happen and I anticipate a difficult situation, I find it hard to breathe.   As I am on my way to the event, I moisturize my mouth with a eucalyptus mint cough drop and sip water. This powerful mint soothes my throat and opens up my nasal passage for full breaths.

If you feel so stressed that you cannot take in a full breath, then you must do some physical exercise like jogging, walking, etc. Do something physical! Go to a garden, forest, or any moving water and walk until your anxiety subsides. You will begin   to   breathe   fully!

Pay close attention to your thoughts! Keep your thoughts flowing from your inspired mind! When you catch yourself holding your breath or breathing fast, consciously breathe your six sets to get to your relaxed mind where your relaxed heart space resides. Remember, our brain uses 20% of all oxygen consumed by our body. Therefore, breathe your way into your new learning experience. Breathing into your relaxed heart space will give you supreme concentration for learning and bring balance into your life. *Breathing deeply can help you to be compassionate to yourself as you develop a balanced life of learning/living through your relaxed   heart   space.*

Notes

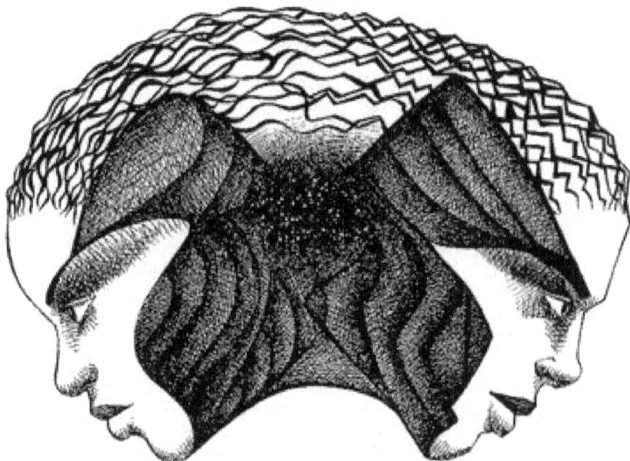

© Kadir Nelson 1993

4

Whole Brain * Whole Mind Power

A mind! We all have one! We all have a magnificent mind, a computer. Our minds are much more brilliant and complete than the computer. We only use one half of one percent of our total mind capacity.

This chapter is dedicated to telling you how to use more of your inspired mind on a mental level, not the physical level. I am not discussing the physical or biological properties of the brain in this book. I'll leave that for the scientists. As shown in the diagram below, the left and right hemispheres of the brain are connected to the opposite sides of the body. Thus, the left eye is connected to the right brain and right eye is connected to the left side of the brain. This demonstrates the physical level.

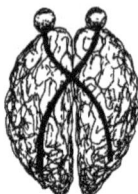

Try this exercise:
- Raise your right leg off the floor.
- Bend your knee.
- Now rotate your foot clockwise.
- While you are rotating your right foot clockwise, use your right pointer finger and draw the Number **6** in the air.

What Happened???? Your right foot switched directions and started going the same direction of counterclockwise like your right pointer finger. A counterclockwise motion draws the number six. Now try this with your left leg and left finger. Did the same thing happen?? WHY? The right side of the body is connected to the left-brain and the left side of the body is connected to the right brain. I have had you demonstrate this for yourself to convince you that you must do something to connect the two sides of your brain. What do you do to connect the two sides of your brain??? BREATHE DEEPLY AND RELAX!!!!

For purposes of clarity, I will describe the left brain that is logical, linear, and analytical as the reasoning mind and the right brain is creative, insightful and calm as the relaxed mind.

Whole mind is the system of using the **relaxed mind** and the **reasoning mind** powerfully integrated for optimum learning through your relax heart space. **Whole mind** learning takes place when the **reasoning mind** receives complete information intuitively from the **relaxed creative mind**. The **reasoning mind** then has the opportunity to use its skill to express this information intelligently. This is the **whole mind** learning experience. The reasoning mind in peace balances with your relaxed mind in your heart space to become your servant to do as you command.

The only difference between any two human beings is the way they use or do not use their **heart space** to process information and events that they see or experience. Now let's learn more about the mind through the **heart space.** Learning from the **heart space** helps you to simplify your life.

"RELAXED HEART SPACE"

This is a place of non-judgment, non-attachment, open mindedness, peace, love, truth, and simplicity. This is a place to just "BE" you. This is a place for pure freedom. This is your relaxed response system.

The **reasoning mind** is the part of your mind that thinks for you and moves your body. It uses your five physical senses to communicate to you what you see, hear, taste, smell and touch as you relate to the environment around you. Most people know the functions of this part of the brain the best. This part of the mind analyzes all the detail and parts of any event, problem, crisis or conflict with the information it has received for you. Your left-brain, reasoning-mind is your short-term memory and a very small percentage of your long-term memory. Information must be repeated 10 times to build a long-term memory block in your reasoning mind. These memory blocks become your habits. Your reasoning mind is **only memory** and cannot create anything new. Your reasoning-mind can re-evaluate and re-analyze the same data with a different perspective, but it is still the same data.

The **relaxed mind** relates to your environment through feelings and intuition. This is the part of your mind where all new ideas are created. Everything that is created in art, music, poetry, computer software, is created in the relaxed mind. Your genetic memory is imbedded in your DNA memory inherited by you from your ancestors of 7,000 generations. You can access this vast information by breathing deeply into your relaxed mind.

Your peace, serenity, special talents, creative genius and long-term expansive memory is accessed through your relaxed mind. When you breathe deeply into your relaxed mind while you are studying, you only have to study **once** then review. Relax and breathe to put the information into your relax mind and relax and breathe deeply to retrieve the information.

Relaxed Mind and Reasoning Mind in Peace

As you look at this model below, you see the different functions of the Relaxed Mind and the Reasoning Mind balanced in peace:

- The whole mind is enhanced by the deep relaxed breathing process.

- Deep relaxed breathing leads to balance in the heart space.
- Your reasoning mind in peace is your trusted servant receiving wisdom from your relaxed mind. This is your Heart Space for learning.

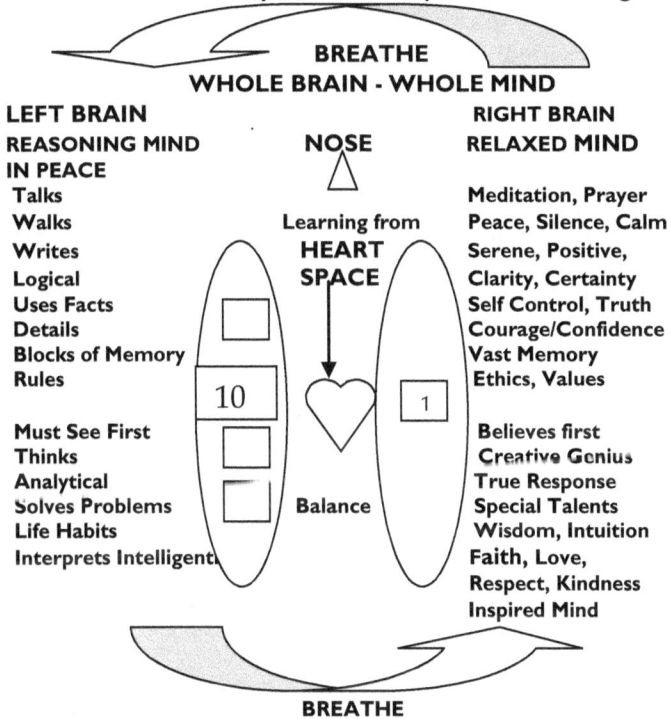

BREATHE
WHOLE BRAIN - WHOLE MIND

LEFT BRAIN		RIGHT BRAIN
REASONING MIND	**NOSE**	**RELAXED MIND**
IN PEACE	△	
Talks		Meditation, Prayer
Walks	Learning from	Peace, Silence, Calm
Writes	**HEART**	Serene, Positive,
Logical	**SPACE**	Clarity, Certainty
Uses Facts		Self Control, Truth
Details		Courage/Confidence
Blocks of Memory		Vast Memory
Rules		Ethics, Values
	10 1	
Must See First		Believes first
Thinks		Creative Genius
Analytical		True Response
Solves Problems	Balance	Special Talents
Life Habits		Wisdom, Intuition
Interprets Intelligently		Faith, Love,
		Respect, Kindness
		Inspired Mind

BREATHE

Reasoning Mind in Stress

What happens to us when we become fearful, doubtful and angry? The Reasoning Mind is cut off from the Relaxed Mind when it is in stress. I am depicting the emergency system as **the wall.** Your emergency response system is usually known as fight or flight. Your emergency system is triggered by problems, conflicts, life situations, panic situations, crises and challenges. At the moment of the emergency you have choices. When people stop breathing they become paralyzed by fear and get stuck behind **the wall** in stress. **To Breathe or Not to Breathe!!** Choose to Breathe and come from behind the wall.

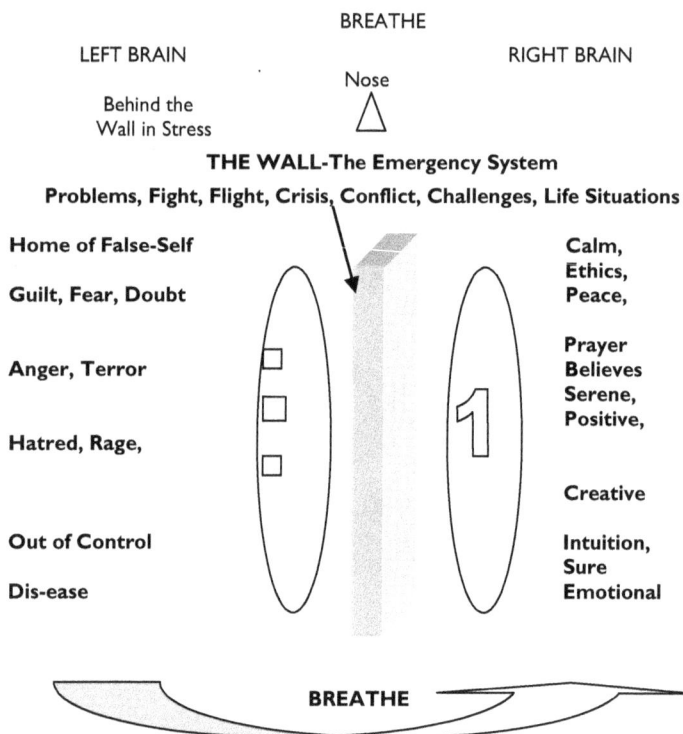

BREATHE

LEFT BRAIN   RIGHT BRAIN

Nose

Behind the
Wall in Stress

THE WALL-The Emergency System
Problems, Fight, Flight, Crisis, Conflict, Challenges, Life Situations

Home of False-Self		**Calm,**
		Ethics,
Guilt, Fear, Doubt		**Peace,**
		Prayer
Anger, Terror		**Believes**
		Serene,
		Positive,
Hatred, Rage,		
		Creative
Out of Control		**Intuition,**
		Sure
Dis-ease		**Emotional**

BREATHE

Whole Mind in Balance

To access the whole mind process, you must choose to breathe deeply at the immediate onset of any crisis, problem, challenge or conflict and continue to breathe until you become relaxed and peaceful to know clearly your resolve.   Next, you move into action without fear, doubt, anger or hesitation. Continue to breathe deeply through your nose and choose not to reverse any of your inspired responses.

You are the master of your mind. Your peaceful pathway to learning is in the power of controlling your mind through your breath to your **heart space**. To move you from behind the wall out of stress, you must breathe to get to your relaxed mind. You breathe to your relaxed mind to correct and refresh the information. Choose to breathe deeply and relax. You will receive an emotional bath of peace, love, compassion and clarity in your relaxed mind. Once you receive clarity of your true response, you breathe to get back to your conscious reasoning mind for action.

Once the challenge or problem is solved, breathe deeply to return your heart space and live and learn peacefully. It is just that simple.

If your first response was **not** to breathe and relax, you will find yourself behind **the wall** in stress. Stop right at that moment of recognition and breathe deeply. Keep breathing until you feel calm coming all over you. Ask yourself at that moment, "How do I resolve this situation?" You will feel your answer from within.

How will you know if you are in stress behind the wall? Your breathing becomes quick and shallow. Your eyes may burn. Your heart rate may speed up. You may fill nauseous. Your head - neck and back may ache. Your hands may become sweaty. You may feel suddenly tired. All these symptoms are signs of FEAR and stress. Fear is the mind killer. Fear paralyzes the mind and the body and then sends you into confusion.

STOP and BREATHE DEEPLY! **Become alert and respond with inspired action.** I encourage you to draw the diagrams in color in your journal to build this memory into your mind. Using color also enhances your retention. When you know this diagram, you will always know where you are in your mind and respond accordingly to any situation. It is also important to know where other people are in their mind before you attempt to respond to them.

What thoughts are haunting you and talking you out of your greatness before you even get started? How many times have you heard the right answers in your mind but "something" talked you out of your wisdom and then continued to upset you? It is a worrier. It is your false ego. It is a stress maker called your false self. Your false self can only talk to you from your past memory. It is limited by past experiences and can never create any new ideas or solutions. Your false self cannot live in the present moment because it can only relate to your past memories. Therefore nothing in your life can change. Your thoughts will be the same every day when you are listening to your false self.

How can I achieve stillness and peace through the power of my breath? Sometimes getting quiet in the mind is not an easy job. Your false-self rules you from your stressed and worried mind behind the wall. Your false self has power over you through your fears, doubts, dysfunctional life habits and insecurities. When you decide you **are** going to meditate and quiet this raging voice in your mind, this false self does not give up its power so

48

easily. When you close your eyes to relax and settle down, this false-self starts to remind you of:

- Your obligations-The things you should be doing instead of relaxing
- The thing you have forgotten to do
- Your bills that need to be paid -And on and on

This false self will even lie!!! It will have you hearing things, feeling like something is crawling on you, hearing doorbells, phones ringing or anything that can trigger you to get up and not get quiet. Your false self is triggered by pride, greed, fear, ignorance and harmful desires. Silence and peace kills the false self in your stressed mind.

As you look at the above brain models, you can recognize the different aspects of the relaxed mind versus the reasoning mind when it is not in stress, and how the reasoning mind acts when it is in stress. Your pathway to learning is in the power of your breath to move you from behind the wall in stress and beyond your reasoning mind into your relaxed mind to receive an emotional bath of peace, love, compassion and clarity. Once peace and clarity are achieved, you breathe back to your conscious reasoning mind for action.

Which frame of mind do you function in the most, reasoning, relaxed or behind the wall? How effectively do you use your mind?

There are times when you must use your emergency system such as fires, car accidents, earthquakes, hurricanes, natural disasters, deaths, etc. Learning is not an emergency situation. You do not need to be in your emergency system on the wall to learn.   **Teachers do not need to put their students in fear to get them to learn.**

You can use your reasoning and relaxed mind effectively as a whole mind for thinking, learning and remembering. All meaningful learning, decisions and thoughts start in the relaxed mind because the relaxed mind has the ability to see the whole picture, access more memory and be creative. The reasoning mind can only see each part. These parts must be repeated 10 times before it becomes long-term memory.   The reasoning mind can only string together boxes of information in a logical, linear and sequential fashion. If there is any information missing or gaps in the data, no matter how you string the boxes of information together you will choose the wrong answers for your conclusion every time.

How do your thoughts affect you? Your mind can only process one thought at a time, either inspired or uninspired. The choice is yours. We process thoughts that create fear or peace throughout the day. Thoughts are energy! Your stressed mind can give you the incorrect information if you are not paying attention and being alert. When you are learning something new, do not let your reasoning mind instruct or move you into action until you have learned all the new parts. Your reasoning mind can be impatient and usually does not have all the data it needs to advise you correctly. If you allow your reasoning mind to advise you at this time, it will guess. I guarantee, it will guess wrong.

Try this. Get 8 color markers and an 8 ½ x 11 piece of white paper. Write the following words in all capitals. Write each word in a **different color** than the **word** it describes. What do I mean? Write the word BLACK in any color but black. Write the world yellow in any color but yellow and so on until all the color words are written down.

Turn the paper over and let your eyes rest for a few seconds.   Turn the paper back over and instruct your mind to:

"SAY THE COLOR NOT THE WORD! "

Having trouble staying focused??   Your reasoning mind is trying to make you say the word and ignore the color even though you consciously told your reasoning mind the instructions: "SAY THE COLOR NOT THE WORD!!" Your reasoning mind is used to only reading the words not saying the color. You have to keep telling your reasoning mind during this exercise to say the color not the word. Since your reasoning mind executes your speech pattern and talks for you, you must make it obey you! You are NOT your reasoning mind. You do not obey your reasoning mind. Your reasoning mind must obey you. It must do what you tell it to do! You are the Master not it. The reasoning mind is your servant. Below is sample of a worksheet to practice.

BLACK YELLOW GREEN

BROWN ORANGE BLUE

PURPLE BLUE RED BLACK

PINK GREEN ORANGE RED

**LEFT BRAIN-REASONING MIND and RIGHT BRAIN – RELAXED MIND
IN FEAR/STRESS –OR- LOVE/PEACE**

BREATHE

WHOLE BRAIN- WHOLE MIND
REASONING MIND LEFT BRAIN

LEFT BRAIN		
RIGHT BRAIN		
REASONING MIND	IN PEACE	RELAXED MIND
BEHIND		
THE WALL		
IN STRESS		△ Nose

THE WALL- The Emergency System
Problems, Fight, Flight, Crisis, Conflict, Challenges

Home of False Self		Peace, Silence, Calm
Guilt, Fear, Doubt	Talks	Meditation, Prayer
Anger, Terror	Walks	Believes first
	HEART SPACE	Serene, Positive,
Hatred, Rage	Writes	Creative Genius
Out of Control	Logical	for Life	Intuition
Stress, Dis-ease	Uses Facts	Sure
Un-forgiveness	Blocks of	Self Control, Truth
Confuses Problems	Memory	Clarity, Certainty
Insecurities, Jealousy	Rules	Ethics
Denial, Revenge	Must see first	Wisdom, Intuition
Pride, Greed	Moves Body	Disharmony,
Misery	Thinks	Values, Morals
Illogical,	Use Senses	Solves Problems
Rigid Rules, Paranoid	Limited	Love, Respect,
	Control	Creative Genius

BREATHE

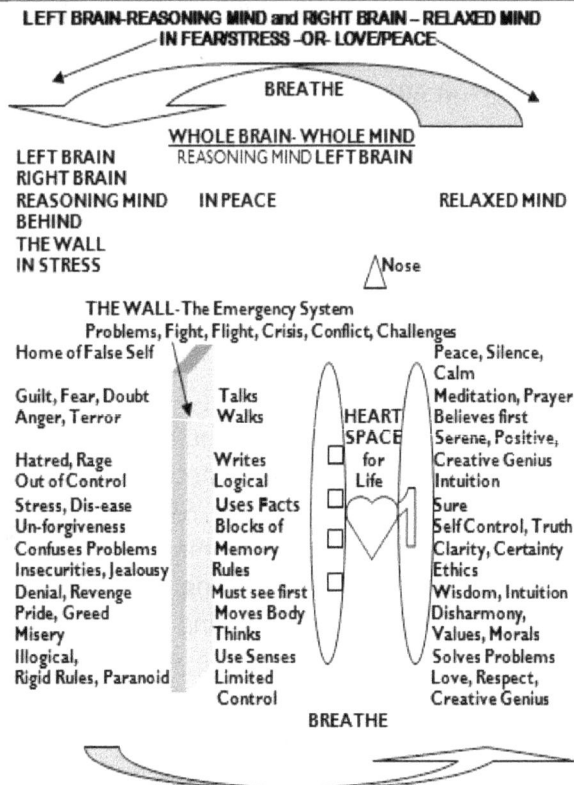

Your reasoning mind creates your memory
and your habits, which become your unconscious
mind. Your unconscious mind is only memory. It can
become and insist on being a tyrant over your life.
Your unconscious mind thinks it knows everything.
Well it does not.   It only knows what you have
stored in it from your past experiences. **Your left-
brain/reasoning mind cannot create anything
new**.   All it can do is shift, re-shift the same data
repeatedly, and continue to come up with varying
solutions with the same data.

How can you choose to live through your inspired mind? How can you choose to use your creative mind first, and then instruct your reasoning mind to flow in rhythm with your body to perform any task? How can you choose to learn without fear? How can you stay relaxed and enjoy acquiring knowledge? How can you instantly retrieve information from your mind? How can you stop putting down the right answer and then talking yourself out of the right answer and erasing it?

How?...By consciously breathing deeply through your nose until you are relaxed and living and learning from your heart space.

Consciously breathe to link to your knowledge.
Consciously breathe to conquer fear, doubt and anger.
Consciously breathe to love, peace and freedom.

"When you conquer fear, doubt and anger, you conquer failure!" I first read this in *As a Man Thinketh* by James Allen, in 1981. This book changed my life. You must see the whole picture first, then in retrospect pull it apart, analyze and believe each component. If you cannot see the whole, then parts can be missing. Something will be left out. When something is left out, you get the wrong answer every time. Once the relaxed mind gives the reasoning mind the whole picture then the reasoning mind can enjoy manipulating all the data and logically and sequentially arrange and rearrange the data for whatever decisions you would like to make or to understand or to conclude.

We can literally talk and think at the same time. Have you ever been talking and had a great thought come into your mind? Where did that thought come from? It came through your relaxed creative mind. It is important when these gems of information are allowed to jump into your mind while you are talking. It is important to write down a key word about that thought so that you can anchor it to you for your later use. When you have finished speaking, you can quickly review the key word and the entire thought will come back to you. The key word is your link to that knowledge.

Our reasoning mind talks for us while our creative mind incubates our questions, seeks the answers and sends responses into our reasoning mind to be included in our discussion.

Consciously breathe to your relaxed creative mind. You will learn easier and faster. You will process massive information better. You consciously breathe to put information in the long-term memory and consciously breathe to retrieve it.

"You Have the Power to Choose Your Level of Knowledge and Wisdom"

You have two personalities, your highest self and false self. Your personality, distinguishes you from the outside world. It allows space for your creative genius and special talents to expand. Your highest self-dwells in your relaxed mind and your heart space. You can trust in yourself and your talents through your heart space.

Your false self builds its house in your destructive daily habits behind the wall of stress. Our habits can be constructive or destructive. Your false self criticizes your dreams Hence, our habits can heal us or hurt us. Many of us have become a robot or a slave to our destructive habits. When our daily habits harm us, our false self is running our life through fear, doubt, anger, lack, guilt and un-forgiveness. Our false self has no compassion for us or anyone else. It can't have compassion, it is only memory. Your false self is a tyrant over your life, demanding that you obey it and live in the past. Living in the past means that you are living through your past mistakes and upsets. This destroys your self-esteem,   self-love   and   self-acceptance.

You are the center of your universe!

Your Thoughts   **Your Feelings**

YOU
Your Family
Your Community
The Rest of the World
And the Universe

Your Actions   **Your Emotions**

How connected are you to all living beings around you? You are not an island. How are you participating or not participating with others around you? Are you being responsible for the space you are holding in the universe? This is your space in which you are to create your life. You create in collaboration with others around you. Is your interaction compassionate? You are the center of your universe. You're every thought, your feelings, your emotions, your words and your actions radiate from you through your family, community, and the world/universe like a bell. When your thoughts, feelings, emotions align in the center in peace, you gain   authority   over   your   life.

Choose to live at the top of your pyramid!

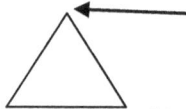

Living a life of learning is a life of living in the present moment. Living in the **NOW** means your mind is clear and open ready to hear your true response from your inspired self. You are then able to respond intelligently with your words and actions. You are able to be compassionate through your heart space.

We must empower ourselves with compassionate thoughts about ourselves so that we can remain on our journey of learning. This is a moment-by-moment opportunity for you. **Now** is the present moment. *The present moment lasts forever*. The present moment never goes away. *All time is now*. Living in the **now** takes practice and can become your good life habit. You get to respond to life with the full presence of Your Spirit, Your Will, Your Heart and Your Body. When you live in the **now**, you get to use your creative geniuses and special talents to support your life forever. ☙❧

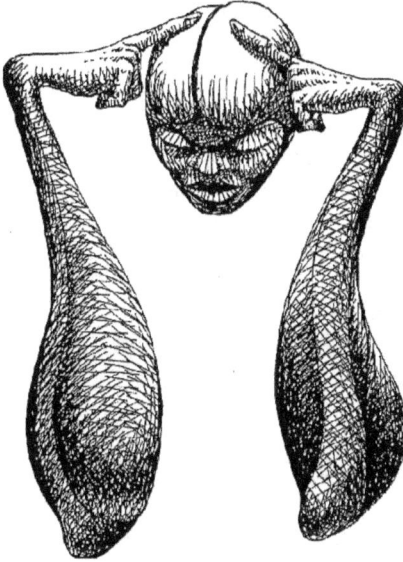

Kadir

©1993
Nelson

5

Creative Geniuses-Talents

"Imagination is greater than knowledge" -Einstein

Every human being was born with vibrations (intelligent energy) of the eight multiple intelligences/creative geniuses to use to excel in and to help them share their talents with the world. Choose now to identify and accept your geniuses. If you can breathe, you can access your geniuses. **No one got left out!!** We are all brilliant in some way. Really, **you have all eight geniuses in you right now** waiting to wake up. Whatever your creative geniuses are, ask yourself, "How can I serve myself and others in my business, career, job, community and family using my geniuses and my special talents?"

In order to be a success with ease and happiness, you must use your creative geniuses and special talents to create right place and time for your life's work.   Let us take a quick peak at the creative intelligences/geniuses that were first described by Howard Gardner in *Frames of Mind*. More information on all eight multiple intelligences can also be found in his book, *Intelligence Reframed: Multiple Intelligences for the 21st Century*.   Your **intelligence** is the way in which you relate to, understand and perceive the world.

This intelligence helps you to process all information coming into your mind. Your reasoning mind is used to processing, understanding, categorizing and assimilating this information. Each of us was born with a certain percentage of the eight intelligences. You can always learn how to use more of each one. I shall give you simple explanations of the 8 multiple intelligences, so that you can self-identify which geniuses you have naturally and which ones you will start to learn how to use more.

What Are the 8 Multiple Intelligences/Geniuses?

1.   Interpersonal/Social Learner = People Smart

These individuals have great ability to understand and relate to others. They have great social skills. They are people oriented and outgoing. They enjoy talking to people, making, and maintaining friends. They are very sociable. They want to talk to everyone. They are very sensitive to moods, verbal and silent dialogues of others.

When they are learning information, they need to ask questions and talk over these ideas with others to process this information. It is important for them to express themselves verbally otherwise; their ability to assimilate and understand the information will be severely limited. Interpersonal people love to raise their hands in class and to participate in study groups. They love group projects. They are not hyperactive. They are passionate about expressing themselves and learning.

Interpersonal people excel in leading, organizing, communicating and mediating. Many of our teachers, politicians, counselors, sales people, public relations personnel, social workers, actors, doctors, lawyers business and religious leaders fall in this category.

2.   Intra-personal/Individual Learner = Self Smart

They are self-motivated, with a great ability to know them. They are self-aware and when they decide they want to share information about themselves, it is evident that they have a great sense of self and have developed a well-planned direction for their life. They reflect on their own thoughts very well. They undertake detailed mental self-examination of their feelings, thoughts, and motives. They follow their instincts and intuitions.

When they are learning information, they go away from everyone else and ponder about what they have learned. They need to process this information alone even if they are sitting in a classroom full of people. They do not participate in class much, but when they speak, it is worth listening to their every word. They do not enjoy group projects. They like working alone on individualized projects. They set personal goals, do original work and like working in a private space. They are intuitive about what they learn and how it relates to them and others. They are intra-personal when they are learning information. When they have completed the learning process and are ready to share this information they use their interpersonal intelligence. It is possible to have 100% of both interpersonal and intrapersonal geniuses.   Many of our teachers,   novelists,   counselors,   psychiatrists, philosophers, healers and   leaders are in this category. People are both geniuses at different times.

3.   Mathematical/Logical Learner – Number Smart

They are great with computers and have great mathematical ability. They like figuring things out. They realize the patterns and related functions of problems. They love doing experiments, solving problems, working with numbers.

When they are learning, their mathematical ability is intuitive at first, then immediately intellectual and logical. They feel the answer, then immediately perform any operation. Those with the mathematical genius are right and left-brained. They use their whole brain. They go into a zone where they become the problem and the solution simultaneously.

To process information, they   always go back to the beginning of a problem and work through any solutions that come into play during the problem solving session.   They fill in the gaps that others would have ordinarily missed. They are great on a team. If allowed, they ask the necessary questions that still have not been asked. Mathematical/Logical learners use their senses of sight, hearing and touch when exploring new possibilities. They must see models to feel the truth inside of them.

Many of our accountants, lawyers, scientists, mathematicians, engineers, architects, designers, astronauts, pilots and detectives fall under this category.

4. Visual/Spatial Learners = Art and Space Smart

These individuals have great creative ability. They think, see and feel dimensionally in color. They love to draw, build, design and create things. They must be able to visualize the information in their mind's eye. Your mind's eye is also called your mental blackboard, inner eye and pineal gland. Many times the spatial/visual learner is accused of daydreaming. They work in their relaxed mind, their right brain first, by picturing the information, and then they transfer this information flawlessly to their left-brain for execution of the information artistically, graphically or with charts. They are great navigators through land, sea and space. They think and feel dimensionally in color. They organize spatially.

They learn well when the information is presented in color and with visual models, with maps, art, illustrations and charts. If they cannot see it in their mind, they will not process the information well. Many times their notes are doodles that they made as the instructor is talking. This means they processed and stored the information very well.

Many of our artists, architects, physicists, navigators, pilots, sculptors, actors, teachers, musicians, surgeons, researchers, sailors, astronauts and marketing strategists are in this category.

5. Musical Learner = Rhythm Smart

These individuals have great musical and rhythmic ability. They remember, create, and recognize melodies, pitches and rhythms well. They like to sing, hum, whistle, listen to music and/or play an instrument. They can turn any object into a musical instrument.

While learning they process information as they move part of their body rhythmically or tap a pencil against the desk. The more they are understanding the information and storing it well in their minds, the more they tap or move rhythmically. They always have a song in their head or a rhythm moving their body.

If you are using background music to learn, teach or study by, be sure to put the music on repeat shuffle to keep changing the pattern of the music, otherwise musical learners will start to hum, sing or anticipate the next chord and become distracted from the lesson. Musicals have sensitivity to pitch, melody, rhythm and tone. Many musicals can easily distinguish one person from another by their voice alone. They also are sensitive to the emotional qualities of music and the human voice, our first musical instrument. These individuals relate to others through their voice and the voice they hear.

Many of our conductors, dancers, performers, composers, musicians, music critics, singers, instrument makers, skilled listeners and recording artists are in this category.

6. <u>Kinesthetic/Bodily Learners = Body Smart</u>

These individuals have great bodily coordination and the ability to manipulate and control objects. Their physical skills are fine-tuned. They have whole body coordination. They use their right brain and left-brain to unite their mind and body into perfect physical movement.

They always have something in their hands when they are learning information. If they are to learn about an object, they touch it, hold it, and walk around with it to process the information. It is important they have hands on models to work with during the learning process. Some of the kinesthetic types move their bodies when they are learning information or they have to stand up. They are not like the musical types who move rhythmically They move sporadically.

Many of our actors, athletes, surgeons, engineers, architects, designers, astronauts, pilots, jewelers, mechanics, inventors, builders, and dancers fall under this category.

7. <u>Linguistic Learner = Word Smart</u>

These individuals have a great ability to read, write, spell, speak and listen. As discussion leaders, they have a great ability to think in words and to use language to express complex meanings. They learn foreign languages easily.

They write down every word they hear when they are learning information. Their notes are the greatest. Many times they do not even need to review their notes before a test because they have already thoroughly processed the information in their minds when they originally took notes. If they are not allowed to write down the information, they will process the information poorly. They are great storytellers.

Many of our poets, writers, orators, public speakers, journalists, novelists, linguists and politicians are in this category.

8. Naturalist Learner = Nature Smart

These individuals have a great ability to understand the relationship and interactions between living organisms and their natural or developed environments. They relate to the natural forces controlling the physical world and the processes that collectively control the phenomena of the physical world independent of human intervention.

They love outdoors, field trips, camping and hiking. They like to be around plants and animals. They can easily recognize and classify flora, fauna, and other objects in nature. They are interested in learning about planets, stars and space. When they are learning, they must feel the answer intuitively first then gather information to prove their theory. They need fresh air and breaks to be outside in nature. Many of our biologists, zoologists, botanists, farmers, veterinarians, marine biologists, pharmacists, medical doctors, and ecologists are in this category.

More detail can be found in Jeanette Voss' book, *The Learning Revolution* and Collin Rose's *Accelerated Learning*. Choose now to identify your creative geniuses. These are your special gifts. These gifts are the foundation of your life's learning and work. A great book I used 25 years ago to identify my gifts and my children's geniuses was *What Color is Your Parachute?", by Richard Bolles.* Choose now to mark out a path for you to achieve using your creative geniuses. Use the information on each creative genius to fill each space on the bar graph to identify your vibration in each genius. Please use a different color for each bar. You can learn to have 100% in all eight geniuses to use when you need!!

8 Creative Geniuses/Multiple Intelligences

0% 5% 25%   50%   75%   100%

INTEPERSONAL

INTRAPERSONAL

MATHEMATICAL

VISUAL

MUSICAL

KINESTHETIC

LINGUISTIC

NATURALIST

ॐ

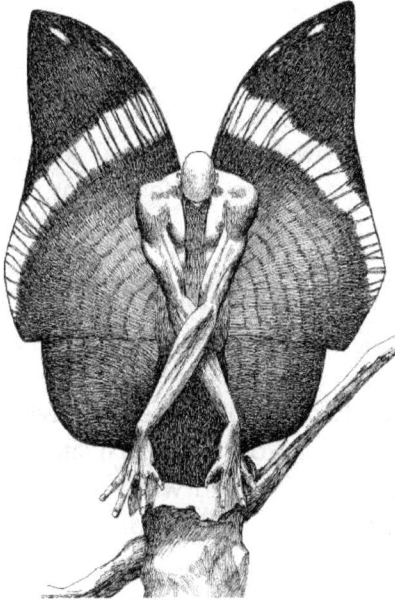

KadirNelson©1993

6

CHOOSE YOUR LIFE IN BALANCE

"What Makes a Balanced Life of Learning?"

Having a balanced life gives you a reason to want to learn and grow. Your pathway to learning with ease is a wonderful journey when you are in balance First, ask yourself, "How, where, when and who can I serve with my special talents. Your balanced journey is accomplished by living through your heart space. This journey will lead you to your balanced life. Enjoy and feel each moment. It is not about the final destination, because you will be learning for the rest of your life. There is no final destination in learning.

Your life is a journey. It is up to you if it is going to be a joyous or miserable trip. You choose who is going to be on this journey next to you. I say next to you, because everyone has his or her own life destiny pathway, even if you are a twin. Each person has his or her own life lessons. To only want to study and do nothing more, you are out of balance. Those people who are close to you, on your path to learning can be a cheerleader or a deterrent. A deterrent is someone who discourages you at every turn. Be careful that you only have people around you who will be your avid supporter.

You chose your personal life values. Please keep those values in mind while you make decisions throughout this section. You completed your Mission Statement and your Goal Statement using these values. If you did not complete your Mission and Goal Statements, I suggest you go back to Chapter 2 and complete it to get the most out of this section. I want to give you more information now to assist you in crystallizing your thoughts and actions that will help guide you to your compassionate pathway to learning.

There are eight components to a balanced life, which will inspire your intense desire to learn more. When any of these parts are left out of your life, your life is out of balance. Learning becomes difficult when your life is out of balance.

The Eight Life Component Parts are:
- **Your purpose in life/your life's work**
- **Your family**
- **Your personal loving relationships**
- **Your education/job/career/business**
- **Your home/transportation**

- **Your personal health**
- **Your personal   growth**
- **Your community, heritage and volunteer time**

The more control and responsibility you have over your life, the more compassionate you can be with yourself and others during your learning processes. You will experience less stress with others when you have more compassion for yourself. When you have compassion for yourself, you do not become frustrated when others want to teach, inform or show you something new or different.

1. Your Life's Purpose-Your Mission in Life

What is your aim in life? What greater purpose do you want to accomplish? We make our living from what we get. We make our lives from what we give. What would you like to give to the world using your personal talents and geniuses? What personal values and ethics will you live by to accomplish this purpose?

You have chosen your personal values. You wrote your Mission and Goal Statements. You identified your creative geniuses. Whatever your capability is, you have a life's purpose to match it. We need to identify the youth's geniuses when they are very young, so that their gifts are not smothered with fear and doubt. When you write down all of your identified creative geniuses, your life's purpose can be identified. All this leads you to a path of joyfully learning more about your purpose and the knowledge you want to achieve in order to be more of a service to yourself and others.

What do you want that money cannot buy? Get quiet and go into your heart space and ask yourself what you would be joyful doing for the rest of your life. If someone gave you $50 million dollars and told you that you could develop any business you wanted as long as you are being of service to others. What business would you build? How you would be of service to others? What life's work would be a joy to your heart? What work would you do for free as volunteer work? All of the answers to these questions will get you closer to your life's purpose.

2. Your Family

Who will be a part of your life five-ten years from now - spouse, significant other, children, extended family and significant relatives? Where will your children be in their lives in five-ten-fifteen years? Record the names of your family members who will be supporting you unconditionally as you achieve your journey to learning and living. What will your spouse or significant other be doing in five-ten-fifteen years? How can you support their journey? If you do not have a spouse or significant other and wish to receive one in your life during this time, just write down the values you want your significant partner to have. If you seek to have children, write down how many.

Many of our hopes and dreams are centered on our families. I am driven by my passion to make this a better world through the personal and spiritual development of the youth, so that my grandbabies will have a better place to live. When you are living with purpose and enjoying your work, your family benefits greatly.

Your family is the most affected by your thoughts, feelings, emotions and actions. Are you creating win-win situations and events for your family as you move forward on your destiny to learning? As you achieve and maintain balance, your family will automatically achieve and maintain balance. You are the center of your family, no matter which position you hold (father, mother, daughter, son, etc.)

3. Your Loving Relationships

Think about your best friends; close family members, buddies, spouse and/or significant other. What would you like these relationships to be like in five-ten-fifteen years? Are these relationships sincere, honest, peaceful and fun? Is each of them courteous, kind and respectful? Your loving relationships are those companions you talk to often. When you talk to each other, you just pick up where you left off. You support one another in everything. Your loving relationships may just be a few individuals. You feel peaceful with your loving relationships. The rhythm between you is balanced, loving and harmonious.

When you are with your loved ones, you are each other's strength. You both have mutual admiration for each other. You are like two stars vibrating together. You share your light together. You laugh together and comfort each other. You are unconditionally compassionate and tender to each other. You grow lovingly together. Your sentiment of love purifies your loved ones' emotional body and vice versa.

Your loving relationships are blessings that have come to you. They are friends of your soul. They are tied to you by a special bond. On your passage to learning you will find yourself gathering these friends of the soul effortlessly. The inter-blending between soul mates creates a warm element of life. Soul mates or twin spirits reflect each other's light. Your companionship brings consummate happiness. Your number one aim is to bring joy and peace to your friends. If those around you, project guilt on you, they do not go into this category. As a matter of fact, they do not fit into your future unless they change their behavior.

4. Your Education/Job/Career/Business

What career will you have in five-ten-fifteen years? Write the details including the salary, title, and satisfaction you will feel. What will your office be like? How will you dress for this position? Do you own the company? When your job and your life's work are the same, you live a balanced life. You can be of service to everyone you meet without discrimination. In five-ten-fifteen years, what do you want to be doing with your time, energy and wisdom? How will you be of service to others with a joyful heart? How will you choose to be of service to humankind?

Will you need further training, education or certification to achieve your dream career or business? What education (if any needed) or experience have you completed during this five-year period to earn the opportunity to have this position or own this business? Plan your life, and then work your plan. Imagine your life's work that you can accomplish without struggle but with joy. Choose what you would love to do. Take one baby step at a time to achieve your goal. Get help with the parts of your jobs that you do not like. Your career is your life's energy. What you put out is what you can get back. Your service and prosperity is your energy circulating.

Now, let's take this thought of a career or business to another level. When you truly want to be of service to humanity, you are being of service to yourself. **Your real full time job is living in the loving nurturing light of your heart, being happy, healing yourself and being love on this planet. Everything else is just an assignment.** You go from assignment to assignment being of service with the love and light that comes through you.

When my son, Kadir Nelson was fourteen years old, an elder artist asked him how he could draw and paint such deep content in his paintings. He answered humbly that his art came through him, and as long as he knew where it came from, he would have his talent forever!

5. Your Home

Imagine your home five years from now as your safe space to live, learn and heal. Please choose to have the energy of your home feel light and open like velvet. I suggest you use the ancient art of Feng Shui to assist you in the placement of your furniture and the colors to adorn your home. Get a simple book on Feng Shui. You will see and feel the difference.

Your home is your place of peace. If this is not true, change it or leave it. Everything in your home must be beautiful to you or useful to you. If it is not, get rid of all that is not beautiful or useful. How do you want your home to feel? How do you want your home to look? How do you want your home to smell? How do you want your home to sound? The more beautiful and harmonious your home is, the better your life will be. Your atmosphere for learning will be greatly enhanced.

There is no passage to learning in the mist of clutter and chaos. Please, un-clutter your life. Your passage may stop right in your closets stuffed with the past. Your pathway may stop right in the piles of newspapers and magazines that you will never read. Clutter steals your energy and vitality. What a cheap way to lose your life. Release attachment to the past by letting go of that STUFF!

Remember to include your transportation when planning your home. Reliable transportation is important. Make the necessary repairs or choose to buy a car. Enjoy sweet aromas in your home through aromatic candles, incense burners and potpourri pots simmering delightful essential oils. Sweet aromas create an environment where you can experience an unfolding of your inner spirit. This unfolding of your inner spirit leads you into the depths of your heart space where your joy for learning resides.

Music creates an environment for learning.

Music is important in setting up a relaxed, comforting environment while you study. Choose the musical instruments and style that brings you joy and peace. Originally, baroque and classical music were thought to be the only music to induce this relaxed state, but there are many beautiful relaxing selections being produced now. I recommend that you start your relaxing breaths before you select your music. Match the rhythm of your relaxed heart rate to the music. Some of the suggested 60 beats per minute Baroque music I have used to write, teach and learn by include:

Adagio
  Albinon
Bach
  Air from Overture #3
  Arioso
  Bist du bei Mir
  Jesu, Joy of Man Desires
  Flute Suite in "E"
  Prelude and Allegro in "E" Flat
  Sheep May Safely Graze
  Sleepers, Awake
  The Goldberg Variations by Marlin Gally
  Brandenburg Concerti by Mainz Chamber
  Orchestra
Beethoven
  Fur Elise
  "Moonlight" Sonata
Canon
  Pachelbel Canon
Debussy
  Suite Bergamasque-Prelude: Moderato
  Clair de Lune: Tres Expressif
  Danse: Tarantelle Stryrienne: Allegretto
  Sarabande: Avec une elegance grave et lente
  La plus que lente
  La Mer: From Dawn til Noon on the Sea
  La Mer: Play of the Waves
  La Mer: Prelude to the afternoon of a Faun
Mozart
  Concerto No. 23 in "A" Major
  Sinfonia concert ante in E-flat Major, K 364:
  Andante
Rachmaninoff's Greatest Hits (CBS, Inc) #1,3,
4,5,6,8

Ravel
Pavanne for a Dead Princess
Svendsen
Romance in G, OP. 26
Tchaikovsky
Elegia, from Serenade for String Orchestra
Vivaldi
The Four Seasons: "Autumn" Concerto
Other suggested 60 beats per minute music I have used to write, teach and learn by includes:
Deep Breakfast by **Ray Lynch**
Best of **Kitaro**
In My Time by **Yanni**
Reflections of Passion by **Yanni**
Piano Music by **Gary Lamb**
Love Themes
A Walk in the Garden
Twelve Promises
Imaginations
Music by **Peter Kater and Carlos Nakai**
Migration
Essence
Compassion
Sound Healing by **Dean Evenson and Soundings Ensemble**

Spiritland by **John Huling**
All music by **Liquid Mind!!!!!**

6. Your Personal Health

What is your health like in five years? How do you feel? Do you have vibrant energy? Are you exercising? Do you get plenty of water, oxygen, fresh fruits and vegetables? Your health is important to your personal growth in order to learn anything.

Your body is mostly composed of water. Please cleanse your body daily by drinking water half your body weight measured in ounces. You just need to sip water all day. There is no need to gulp large volumes of water and over-impact your system. Sipping the water will prevent you from having to run to the bathroom all day. Squeezing fresh lemon juice in your drinking water helps to cleanse the inside of your body and raises your vibration.

Exercise is one of those things that everyone says they are going to do but never get to it. Without exercise, our body functions poorly. We lose vitality and strength. Choose an exercise that is easy for you and gives you good results. Walking is one of the many effective exercises.

Get plenty of sleep so your body can replenish itself. Spraying your pillow with a lavender mist will help you to have restful sleep. Massaging your hands and feet at night before you go to sleep will help you to have restful sleep also.

7. Your Personal   Growth

What is your personal value system like in five –ten-fifteen years? What is your   health like in five years?   Are you relaxed, free and satisfied? What have you done during those five years to be at this level of personal growth? Do you have high self-esteem? Your personal growth is your personal responsibility. Your personal growth time is a silent time for you and your heart space.

Your highest self is always there no matter what. When you choose to go into your silence, you have the opportunity to hear your own brilliance. When you hear your brilliance, I want to encourage you to write down these thoughts in a journal or notebook. You will be able to track your personal development as you go back to review your journal or notebook.

Start adding to your personal library by reading the authors who amplify the deep thoughts that churn inside your being. By reading, you meet many wonderful people who share their passion and knowledge unconditionally. Reading also exercises your mind. You get to hear your own opinions, especially when you do not agree with the author. Reading helps you to want to know more about everything. Schedule peaceful playtime for yourself. This is the time to pamper you.

Warm bubble baths sprinkled with rose petals (Men also!!)

At the end of your bath squeeze the rose petals on to you. The essential oils of rose have the highest vibratory level of all flowers. Enjoy:

- Peaceful meditations in beautiful gardens.
- Walks by natural bodies of water.
- Walks in a garden/forest.

Your quiet time is spent in silence. Create a beautiful place in your heart space where you can go every time you want to be alone in silence with your heart.

8.   Your Heritage, Community and Volunteer Work

Within the heart of your community, I encourage you to enjoy your own heritage without apology or regret. The more we enjoy our own culture, the more compassionate we are of others enjoying their authentic culture. America needs to become a stew pot, not a melting pot. Each person must keep his or her own identity and individuality. The best way to live and strive in any culture is to maintain your own. What a more interesting place this would be if every person learned to live his or her heritage, and teach it to others.

Let your heart be your guide where and with whom you volunteer your time. Celebrate your life through serving others. Your volunteer time may be the source of your true life's work and final career. A word of caution: your desires must be something that your conscious mind will accept. Feel free to use your written Mission and Goal Statements as living documents. That means, you can change the contents of your dream at any time by choosing a different life, life-style, or by enhancing the one you have chosen.

When your false self or someone else's false self sends you behind the wall in stress by criticizing your dreams and you feel discouraged, stop all destructive thoughts by breathing deeply six times and say to you:

"I am now abundantly supplied with all the love, time, energy, money, wisdom, peace and compassion to accomplish all that

my heart desires in truth, simplicity and love for myself and all humanity."

Let's explore some of the parts of this visual goal setting statement.

"**I**" – The "**I**" in this statement is **YOU**! You are responsible for yourself and your thoughts, actions and life. Say: "I am responsible, reliable and determined to accomplish all that I desire!"

"NOW" – Stopping and holding on to experiencing "now" is like trying to catch the wind! You can only experience the present moment. Live in the present moment in your heart space. All we have is now! Don't live in the past or the future. Live in the **now**, the present moment. Do your long range planning for the future. Record it as part of your mission and goal statement. Then leave it alone, and **let the process happen.** Stay alert, breathe and respond in each moment appropriately with your heart. Use your mind to be creative on the spot. Live in the now!

"HAVE" – Everything already exist. It will come from wherever it is at the moment. You don't have to ask for anything. Just AFFIRM IT, CALL IT FORTH AND GRACIOUSLY RECEIVE IT IN PEACE.

"ALL"- Please do not limit yourself. You have the right to graciously receive ALL that you affirm and call forth. Only your false self, your left-brain behind the wall in stress will stop you. Breathe and receive ALL that you affirm.

"TIME" – You have the rest of your life to accomplish your goals. If you die tomorrow, you had the rest of your life! We do not know how long the rest of your life is, so start now! Whatever it is that you are to accomplish, you have enough time. *Indecision and the lack of major purpose is the biggest thief of time*. Start now! Choose to enjoy living your major purpose in life now!

"ENERGY"— I heard Les Brown say "When you wake up in the morning, if you can look up, get up!" And I add, "Get up and do something, anything, toward accomplishing the goals that you have seen in your mind's eye. Breathe and relax! You have enough energy! Your energy is your power. Your power is your love. The only place and time that you have energy to manifest what you want is in the present moment. Otherwise, you are using your own energy from your body, which leads to disease.

"MONEY"— Money is relative to how well you use your special talents and geniuses. Money is relative to your energy and your persistence to obtain what you desire. Do not give up. You will be paid for the energy you use to be of service to the community and the world, and then it is up to you to accept money for your services. Life is like a pendulum, what you put out comes back. You put out great service, great wisdom, great energy, then for your services charge a reasonable fee, accept payment and say thank you! Make sure each transaction is a win-win for all involved.

"We make our living from what we get, but we make our lives from what we give."
-Winston Churchill

I add to this profound statement, "To give and get with the same service, will give you a very balanced and fulfilled life!

"WISDOM" – The Superlearning techniques shared throughout this book demonstrate that you have the opportunity to tap into the wisdom you need through your deep breathing into your relaxed mind as you live from your heart space.

"COMPASSION" - To be tender and kind to yourself and others as you begin to manifest the life of your choice is essential to having that life. To be compassionate helps you to ensure that each new event is a win-win for all involved.

Once you have written down these details for your life, put your journal somewhere that you know you can review it often. It is important that you are not anxious about your future, which is tomorrow. You have chosen your future. Now you can let it go. Your reasoning mind has a clear picture of its mission, a clear picture of what it is supposed to accomplish for you. Now you can give all your attention to the present moment, the now. Your reasoning mind cannot function or work for you on yesterday's events or tomorrow's events, only on today. CHOOSE NOW! Napoleon Hill taught us that anything that our minds can conceive and believe, it can achieve.

Begin with the end in mind. The end is what you want to accomplish. The end result is a balanced life, where you will enjoy learning new ideas and thoughts every day. We cannot fully understand the beginning until we see the end. The end is the goal we desire to achieve. Make a commitment to yourself to:

"Decide on what YOU think is right and stick to it!"   --George   Eliot

Decide: **WHO** you want to **BE, WHAT** you want to **ACCOMPLISH and WHAT** you want to **HAVE**. Once you have decided your goals you have a reason for living and especially a reason for **LEARNING!**   You must choose to help yourself. This process is also called goal setting. No one should choose for you. You will be unhappy and unsatisfied when others make choices for you. Take a deep breath!! If you don't know exactly what you want, imagine what it would be if you did!! Just make it up!! Choose a life that feels good to you. People remain locked in their present unfavorable conditions when they are not willing to be responsible for their choices even though they are anxious to improve themselves. Congratulations on the life you are choosing. You have recorded your future on your Mission and Goal Statements. You have empowered yourself to accept your future. You are doing something every day toward your future. You now have a reason to want to learn. You now see, you are a vital part of society and that you have a special gift to give to yourself and the world. Now, let's learn more on how to learn.

❦❧

Notes:

©1993 Kadir Nelson

7

Pre-Read to Access More

Pre-Reading*Speed Seeing
Speed Reading*Speed Recording

You have learned how to breathe deeply to calm your thoughts and prepare your mind for learning. Now I will give the information you need to practice the skills of learning. I will give you the tools necessary to be able to materialize the goals you have set for your Life in Balance.

Before we start, try this exercise. Read the words written in bold below quickly then cover the words. **FINISHED FILES ARE THE RESULT OF YEARS OF SCIENTIFIC STUDY COMBINED WITH THE EXPERIENCE OF MANY YEARS OF EXPERTS**

Remember; cover the words before your read any further.

How many "F's" were in that sentence? Don't look back!!! What answer did you get? 2, 3, 4, 5, or 6? Test your friends. See how varied the answers are. Go back now and reread the sentence and count the "F's" again. The answer is seven. How?? The "F's" that sound like the "F in Fish", your brain readily recognizes. The "F's" that sound like "V in OF", the brain refuses to let you recognize as an "F". WHY?

This is called: "SCOTOMA". Scotoma is the process of your left-brain being programmed to think and respond certain ways under certain conditions, no matter what the eyes actually see. It is important to have you feel this fact that there are times that what you actual see is not translated to you by your left-brain. Speed-reading is a right-brain process. Actual reading is a left-brain process.

What is Speed-reading?

Speed-reading is pre-reading, speed-recording then speed-seeing. It is the process of seeing whole sentences, paragraphs and pages at one time. It is the process of speed recording all that your eyes see. Our relaxed creative mind (right brain) is a powerful video recorder, which stores all this information in our long-term memory. Take note! I said our relaxed mind is the video recorder. You actually take a photo of each page. You must breathe deeply before attempting this process. The technique I am sharing with you is a relaxed mind process.

The Pre-Reading * Speed-Reading Skill:

The pre-reading process starts with six relaxing deep breaths. This breathing will open your relaxed mind to where your long-term memory exists. Once relaxed, you are ready to focus your mind on the subject matter. Drink 4 ounces of water to help your mind become more focused.

1. Focus your mind. If the cover of the book were blank you would not be able to center your mind on the subject at hand. So read the front, back, cover, the table of contents, and the index. This overview gives your mind the opportunity to format your memory banks with the major categories to be included. This overview also gives your reasoning mind the opportunity to read all the parts it gets to reason with later.

In general, the Introduction of a book is important because many of the authors gives commentary on what the purpose of the book is, what format it may be written in, and other revealing information which will give you foresight as you read the book.

2. **Question your mind?** "What is it that I am going to learn from this book?" **The answer is always in the question.** If you cannot ask a clear concise question about what you want to know, you cannot get an answer, especially from your own mind. Your left-brain wants to know why it must read this information. Focus your reasoning mind by affirming the data it's going to receive.

3. **Scan-first snapshot.** You are now ready to take your first snapshot of the book, which I call **scanning**. Scan in the entire book. Run your

pointer finger from the top of the page to the bottom of the page quickly. You use your finger to train your eyes to see. Start at the top of the page and scan to the bottom of the page. You are training your eyes at first to follow your finger down the page and focus faster at the same time. Continue to breathe deeply and comfortably. Go as fast as you can as long as the words are clear and not blurry.

Push yourself at the beginning stages of developing your scanning speed-reading skill. You want to see how fast you can go and still focus clearly on the whole page. Say the word 'zip.' By the time you finishing saying the word zip, you have obtained the optimum speed of your finger running from the top of the page to the bottom of the page.

Go back to the beginning of this book and scan in this entire book, and then come back to this section. Fun, wasn't it?

So now you have a preview of what is to come in the next chapters. From this point on, scan everything you are about to read before you actually read it. Your comprehension will heighten. You will enjoy reading much more. You will come to conclusions faster, and make decisions faster because you have given your relaxed creative mind the whole picture ahead of time. Many times we start to draw conclusions about a situation before we have taken the time to read all the facts.

Before doing research you can scan books in the library quickly and decide which books you want to use. Scan every test before you take it. Your mind is a calculator. Your mind will calculate how long you have to do each item on the test. Have you ever started a test and about halfway through you wanted to know how much further you had to go before you were through? Then you found out that the hard part was yet to come with only one-quarter of the time left! If permitted, scan the test first and that won't ever happen to you again. Scan everything first. At the beginning of each school year, semester, or course, scan in the entire book for each going to learn is gone. Your mind has the opportunity to see the whole book. Now all the mystery and fear of what you think you are going to see is gone and your mind can set up categories in the long-term memory.

4. Skim-Second snapshot. You are now ready to take your next snapshot. This is called skimming. Take your pointer finger and just as quickly run it across the first sentence of each paragraph. Be sure to stop at the first period. You are training your eyes to stop automatically at the first period of each paragraph. Today, most books, newspapers and magazine can be skimmed. That means that the first sentence explains what the whole paragraph is all about. The only people who will read whole articles all the way through are those who need to know more information on that subject.   This is a great tool for research also. You can skim through each text to decide if the information is appropriate for your use. When taking a test, scan then skim the test. As you read each question, hear the answer in your mind and quickly write down a key word in the margin. When you are ready to record the answer on the test, look at your note in the margin and match it with the correct answer.

5.   Continue to breathe deeply and remain relaxed during the entire process. People who love to read recognize that they are very relaxed while reading. While you read, your relaxed creative mind records into your long-term memory and gives you full interpretation of the material. You relax and breathe to put the information in. Therefore, you must relax and breathe to retrieve the information as well.

Now you have turned your mind on to acquire more knowledge. Your mind has formatted your memory banks to retrieve data. You are now ready to read the full material and take notes, if appropriate. There is so much information to read today, that you do not have to fully read everything that comes across your path. As you read I encourage you to use the mind-mapping process in the next chapter to actively take notes once and organize the information at the same time. In review, pre-reading, speed-reading is speed-seeing and speed-recording into your long-term memory in your relaxed creative mind.

Pre-Reading * Speed-Seeing
Speed-Recording
Speed-Reading Summary

In review, speed-reading is speed seeing and speed recording into your long-term memory in your higher mental right brain. The steps are:

1. Deep breathe six sets, drink water and relax.

2. Focus the mind by reading the cover, table of contents, introduction and index.

3. Questions your mind, "What is it that I am going to learn from this book?"

4. Scan using your finger running down the page. Scan in the whole book, text or test.

5. Skim using your finger to read the first sentence of each paragraph quickly. Skim in the whole book.

6. Stay relaxed during the process. Relax to put information in and also relax to get information out of your long-term memory.

∞⧉∞

Note:

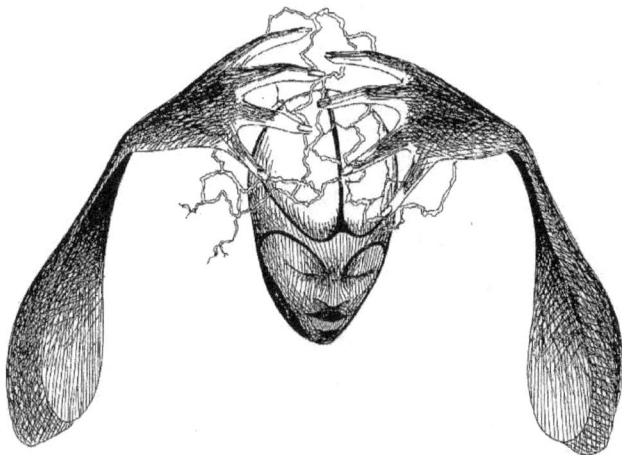

© 1993 Kadir Nelson

8
Mind Mapping- Note Taking

The next skill is the art of randomly recording ideas that flow from your mind and your studies. The end product is totally organized logically notes. This skill will allow you to take notes from many books, and be concise and organized by subject, topic and subtopic in the end. This note taking skill is called Mind-mapping. During mind-storming sessions this skill will empower you to retrieve from your mind a wealth of knowledge while recording this knowledge in an organized fashion.

Tony Buzan of the UK developed the Mind-mapping technique in the 70's and published, *Make the Most of Your Mind (February, 1984)*. This is a circular outline that is read counter-clockwise the same way positive polarity energy flows. Mind-mapping assists you with goal setting. A wish is <u>what</u>

you want to have and do. A wish is only a wish until you write it down, then it becomes a goal. A goal is how
you are going to achieve what you wish. Your reasoning mind now has a road map, a chart to follow. Now your reasoning mind can become like a heat-seeking missile to seek and help you to obtain your goals.

Mind-mapping is a right brain/relaxed mind process of creating new ideas in your mind rather than cramming information in. Mind-mapping facilitates whole mind use by sharing these creative ideas from the relaxed mind for the reasoning mind's use. The key words listed on the mind-map triggers the relaxed mind to give the complete thought. After the whole thoughts are recorded, the reasoning mind can logically and sequentially decide on any conclusion. Mind-mapping helps you to see the whole picture. Mind-mapping helps you to start with the end in mind.

A wish is only a wish until you write it down, and then it becomes a goal.
This leads to your reality.

Mind-mapping is an effective brainstorming tool. **Brainstorming** is the process of opening your mind with others to get new and creative ideas out. Each person participating must breathe to their relaxed mind where their creative ideas are. When each person shares their ideas, their ideas flow freely without judgment or criticism by anyone in the group. Each person is not to judge or criticize his or her own ideas. **Mind storming** is the same process with your own mind and ideas.

Create your mind-map?

Mind-mapping is most useful while retrieving information from many books in which you are researching a specific topic. I will first show you the note taking procedure most of you are familiar with, an outline.

Title/Central Theme

A. Topic
      1. Key sentence about the subtopic
      2. Key sentence about the subtopic
      3. Key sentence about the subtopic

B. Topic
      1. Key sentence about the subtopic
      2. Key sentence about the subtopic
      3. Key sentence about the
subtopic…Etc.

Now see what this same outline looks like on a mind-map. You can literally turn pages and pages of linear notes into one mind-map. Now   let's explore how to create your own mind-map. NOTE: The way you uniquely draw your mind-map is up to you. Everyone has his/her own style. Once you decide how to put the line on the paper, the rest is easy.   This is a simple way of clustering ideas together, as the ideas flow to you randomly. This is a circular outline that is read counter-clockwise; the same way positive energy flows. Mind-mapping is an adventure into your mind's thoughts and power.

You draw a circle about the size of a nickel in the middle of the page and draw eight lines from the circle like the sun. Below is an example of the key principles in the Superlearning 3000 process on a mind-map.

Building Your Mind Map

1. First put your Theme, Major Subject in the middle circle.

2. Draw 8 lines from the middle circle, like the sun.

3. Format your mind-map by putting the major topic on top of each main line. If you are mind-mapping a chapter of a book, you may choose all the headings in that chapter.

NOTE: If you have eight questions to answer at the end of the chapter, you may want to put the questions on each topic line. As you read the chapter record key words to the answer under each line.

4. The last step is to put key words under each topic line on subtopic lines as you read.

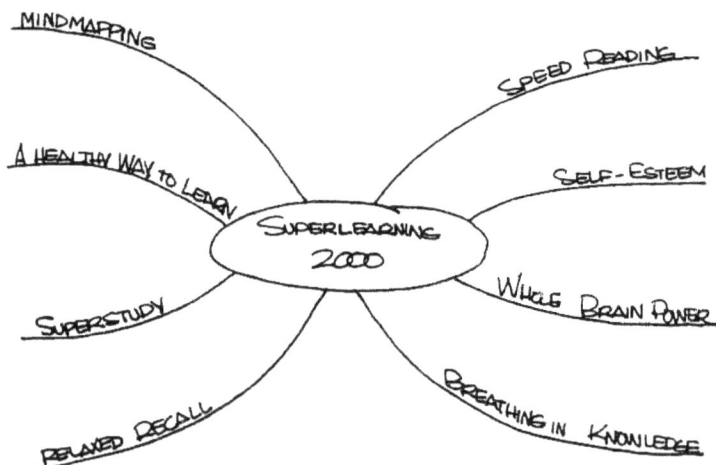

NOTE: You only need key words because you are using your relaxed mind, which only needs key words to trigger the whole thought from your long-term memory.

I suggest that you prepare your mind-maps on 5"x 8" index cards. Index cards are durable and can be used like flash cards when reviewing for a test. I also suggest that you breathe deeply and read your mind-maps **four times**. By the fourth time, your mind is saturated with the information. A **mind-map is read from the bottom right corner around counter-clockwise.** By the fourth time, your mind will speed-read your mind-maps because your mind already has the information stored in your long-term memory.

Mind-maps are formatted the way our brains store information. Your brain stores information in clusters. Each line of your mind-map has similar information clustered around and on it.

We think randomly not linearly when creating and brainstorming. With brainstorming and mind storming, your ideas can flow and be recorded randomly on the mind-map and be organized upon completion of the session you are organized. Start mind-mapping today and you will benefit by:

❑ Having effective recall of the information you have learned
❑ Minimizing the steps it takes to learn
❑ Minimizing the amount of information to be processed
❑ Organizing your thoughts quicker
❑ Coming to conclusions faster
❑ Being more productive
❑ Brainstorming effectively
❑ Mind storming effectively

Other Applications and Uses of Mind-maps

The uses of mind-maps are endless. Whatever you come up with in your imagination can be crystallized into reality through refining your desired solution in a mind storming session while recording the results on your mind-map. **A problem well defined is on its way to being solved. The answer is always in the question. A wish is only a wish until you write it down**. Now your reasoning mind knows the task to perform with clear detail.

Mind-mapping gives structure to listening and assists with a systematic approach to learning. Mind-maps assist you in working progressively toward a solution. Mind-mapping encourages open, interesting ways of thinking. Mind-mapping gives you a step-by-step effective approach to problem solving. List makers try mind-maps on for size. Enjoy!! Dust off your dreams! It is time to make those dreams come true. **First you must have a dream to have a dream come true.** Your life in balance mind-map is a dream that can become your reality by actively pursuing each part of your plan.

A mind-map is read from the bottom right corner<<<< around<<<<< counter-clockwise.

Create your personal Life in Balance mind-map. Record the components parts on each topic line. Let's explore more of your wants and wishes for your passage to learning. Before you start creating your Life in Balance Mind-map, decide if this is a one, five or ten-year plan.

Mind-mapping is a clear and simple way to tell yourself what you want to accomplish. This mind-map is your window to the future to look through. As you create a mind-map with the details of your life on it, in effect, you can follow your pathway to learning. Your mind-map helps you to build energy in the field of all possibilities in life and apply now.

You can set up achievable goals with a mind-map. First, complete your one-year mind-map, and then create more mind maps from this one with more baby steps in it for the day, week or months. As you check off each completed item, you gain a sense of achievement and success. You have more control over your life by proactively choosing your steps. For now, let's take baby steps for a one-year plan. Place your Mission Life Values on the first line to get started. Enjoy the life you create from the inside.

Put main idea in the middle and the projected date for the fruition of this part of your journey. You will want to review this mind-map throughout the years to see how you are doing. You can enhance it at any time. It is a living document. The life in balance mind-map puts your dreams in action. When dreams inspire your life, you have a reason to learn.

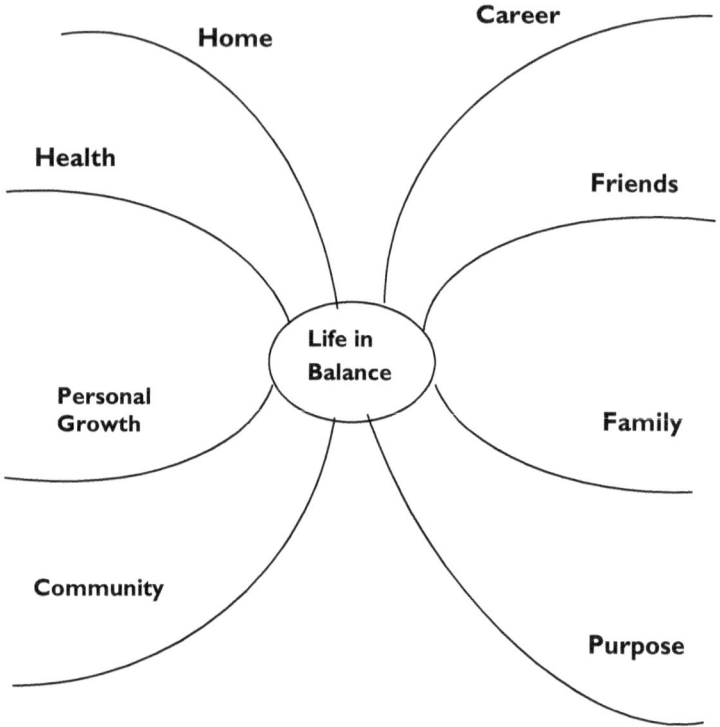

©1993 Kadir Nelson

9

Sleep Incubation Study
"Got Problems-Sleep On It!"

The study technique I am introducing encourages knowledge to flow through you instead of cramming information in.   This technique of studying is proactive learning through self-empowerment, instead of reactive learning out of fear. I want to share a short story with you about how I came up with this technique.

During my college years as a mathematical-statistics major at the **American University in Washington, D.C.**, I was one of the Math Department's tutors. When I needed to be tutored or needed help with my homework, I had no peers to turn to or call. Professor office hours were never during the times that I needed. So I had to go inward and consult with my higher self to get the answers. The only other assistance I had was music of

Rachmaninoff's Greatest Hits to keep me focused and relaxed to get to my math solutions. After laboring for hours on one differential equation problem I would end up-with a near perfect answer, but near perfect was not good enough. I would go to bed with the questions on my mind, "Where is my error?" "Why am I coming up with the incorrect answer?"

At about 2:30AM my mind would wake me up! I would know where the exact error appeared in the problem. I would see on my mental blackboard how to correct the answer all the way to the end of the problem. Many of these problems would go on for several pages. I would complete the problem perfectly and go back to sleep totally amazed, extremely happy and satisfied. The rest of my college experience I never struggled to get the correct answer in mathematics. I would literally "sleep on it." I let my mind incubate and give me the answer when it was ready. I never tried to force an answer out of my mind.

Unfortunately, during my college years, I thought this process was only good for mathematics. I have come to find out from my math students at Grossmont College in San Diego that you do not have to struggle for any great, perfect answers to solutions on any subject. Your relaxed creative mind has the exceptional capability to incubate any idea and give you solutions. This process of mental incubation works for all subjects, events and life situations.

It is important that you ask your relaxed mind precise questions. Ask one question at a time. When I went to bed worrying and failed to ask my relaxed creative mind the questions on my problems, I would not get an answer. When I went to bed stressed and tense, I would get no answers and I would wake up very tired. When I relaxed, asked my questions to be solved, let go and peacefully slept, solutions flowed!

I invite you to have a great life of retrieving creative ideas and receiving knowledge. The ideas you get from the sleep incubation are excellent and valuable. These ideas are worthy of being trusted. When you wake up and drink water, the answers or information you asked for the night before are in waiting.

You can ask your highest self any question before you go off to sleep and hear the answer in the morning. Just drink a glass of water upon waking and information will start to flow through and out of you. Be prepared with a blank mind-map to record key points. That is why when you "sleep on it" you get perfect answers in the morning. While you sleep, your false self and/or your reasoning mind are shut down, allowing your highest self and your relaxed mind to clear the noise and receive the right information on your concerns.

You can incubate your thoughts or questions on life at night while you sleep. Now apply this sleep incubation to the study technique formula. The parts of this formula are a composition of all the skills I have given you. Let us explore why each part is an important part of this successful study formula for learning.

Prepare your study area for learning

The environment you study in can make this learning experience much easier, more exciting and enlightening. You actually enjoy studying when you have all the books and supplies in one well lit area. You look forward to those moments of learning instead of dreading them because you will feel better. You feel good. Study in the same place as often as possible. Your mind automatically knows what purpose and goal you want to accomplish when you sit in your special study place. Your mind will immediately focus on your goals that you have mind-mapped. Your mind will open up to receive the information you are about to learn. Your mind knows that this is the foundation to your future. I congratulate you on the choices you have made to achieve your goals and your dreams. I congratulate you for choosing now!

When you prepare to study, you must first prepare your mind to give and receive creative ideas and knowledge. First, choose which 60 beats per minute music or Baroque music that best relaxes you. Start your breathing while you are preparing your health break snacks and setting up your study area. As the music begins to play, start your conscious breathing. Breathe in through your nose (tickle those hairs in your nose with oxygen to turn on your relaxed creative mind switch) to the count of seven. Hold one count and breathe out through your mouth to the count of 7. Remember, until you are unconsciously breathing deeply this way, count to make sure you are inhaling fully and exhaling fully. Continue to breathe deeply until you are in your relaxed creative mind. You now feel relaxed, peaceful, focused and open to learn.

Bring your health snacks, water, juice and tea to your study area. Make it easy to refresh yourself while studying. Have all the study aids set up in this area.   Study aids may include your textbooks, workbooks, class notes, pens, pencils, 5"x 8" index cards, etc. Have all the essential things you need to complete your studying or project. Good lighting is essential.   Good lighting is about 30 LED watts of light.

Your posture is important to your process of learning also. Keep your spine straight. When you begin to feel tired while studying, hold your head up. Sit up straight and breathe deeply.   Put your shoulders back and smile. You will immediately feel better.

***Focus** your mind on the subject at hand. Do one thing at a time.

***Scan** in all information to be reviewed or studied at that time. At the beginning of each school year, semester, or course, scan in the entire book!

***Skim** in all information to be studied.

***Read** and take notes onto your **mind-maps**.

***Review** your mind-maps three times.

***Prepare to sleep** and **incubate** the material you would like to fully comprehend, retain and recall. In the past, you have heard the following expressions:

"Let me sleep on it."

"Let me take this under consideration."

"Let's shelve this until tomorrow."

Many have found that when the mind has an opportunity for a break, the problem seems clearer. Prepare to receive your solutions in the morning by placing a glass of water next to your bed with a blank mind-map.

If you are very tense and cannot relax before you go to sleep, you can do the following relaxation exercise to prepare your body to sleep peacefully. Lay on your back with a little head elevation. Tense your right leg, raise it up about one foot, and then let it drop. Say to you, **"This is tense."** When each part of your body is up then say, **"This is relaxed,"** as each part of your body is down and relaxed. Next, do this process for the left leg, abdomen, chest, right/left arm, face and then the whole body at once. Now you are ready to breathe into your relaxed creative mind.

Consciously breathe to your relaxed mind. Scan in all the mind-maps you wish to store into your long-term memory. **Read your mind-maps counter-clockwise.** Drift off into a relaxed and peaceful sleep. Upon waking, consciously breathe to your relaxed creative mind. Then drink a glass of water to turn on your reasoning mind. The water will trigger your reasoning mind to receive and record the information that your relaxed creative mind has incubated and combined all night into perfect form for you. You will hear your awaiting thoughts as soon as you begin to wake and begin your deep breathing.

Record the key words of this information onto your mind-map. The key words of this information that are in your long-term memory will come forth from your relaxed mind. Information is coming so fast that you only have time to record key words. When the flow of information has stopped, then you can continue breathing deeply and record full text if you desire. Remember to take **breath breaks** every 20 minutes to refresh your signal to your relaxed mind. Take full 10-minute breaks every hour and a half. One last point, the more senses you use during the learning process, the more you are empowered to turn your dreams into reality by this study process.

The Successful Superlearning 3000 Study Formula for Learning

- Put on your relaxing music.
- Prepare your study area and environment for learning
- Prepare your health break snacks and water.
- Consciously breathe to your relaxed creative mind.
- Focus your mind on the subject at hand.
- Scan in all information about to be learned.
- Skim in all information about to be learned.
- Read and take notes on your mind-maps.
- Read mind-maps three times.
- Prepare to sleep incubate.
- Do relaxing exercises.
- Consciously breathe to your relaxed creative mind.
- Scan in all mind-maps to be studied.

- Drift off into a relaxing, peaceful sleep.
- Upon waking, consciously breathe to your relaxed creative mind.
- Drink a glass of water to trigger your reasoning mind to get information incubated in your relaxed creative mind.
- Record key words of the information on your mind-maps.
- Note-Doing your homework is practice. Practice doesn't make perfect, it makes the information PERMANENT!!

PRACTICE MAKES PERMANENT.
Home work is practice.
HOMEWORK MAKES IT PERMANENT.

1993 Kadir   Nelson

10
Relaxed - Recall -Test Taking Without Fear

The ultimate experience in learning is the ability to recall the information easily you believe you have learned. Nothing is more rewarding than the knowledge that all your study efforts are paying off. This study technique is a   proactive approach to learning.

Superlearning 3000's step-by-step approach to learning prepares you for the final event, the exam- the test! This is your opportunity to allow the information you have stored in your long-term memory to flow from you with ease. There is no need for you to force the information out of you. You must just be open to receive the answer when you ask for it by breathing deeply.

You breathe to access your long-term memory. You scanned and mind-mapped the information, you reviewed your mind-maps three to four times, then you incubated this information while you slept peacefully in your relaxed creative mind where your long-term memory resides. During this whole process, you were not guessing at answers, recording misinformation or wrong information. Your mind only had the opportunity to learn and record the right answers. Your mind had the opportunity to condense and compress this information with everything you have ever learned, so that you have full understanding of the total concept. There are no gaps of information missing in this process.

Therefore:

> *You have only learned one answer!*
> *You have only stored the right answer!*
> *You will only know one answer!*
> *You will only know the right answer!*

Believe in yourself and your abilities! There is no need for guessing. You have prepared well to take the test. Your relaxed creative mind will tell you the correct answer every time. My students have described what it feels like when the right answer quickly comes into their mind during a test or throughout their day. They say it **feels like air!**

They say if feels as light as a feather. Why? Wrong answers carry a lot of emotion, because the reasoning mind will throw you behind the wall into emotional stress. This stress happened when there is a gap in the information or you <u>guessed</u> wrong! That is why it is important to ask your relaxed creative mind first for the answers, and then feed this information to your reasoning mind.

The reasoning mind has limited blocks of facts in its very small percent of long-term memory, while the relaxed creative mind has vast knowledge in its long-term memory. Therefore, when the reasoning mind has the complete correct information from the relaxed mind, the answers come like air, light as a feather and free of emotional stress. You get a quiet sense of knowing satisfaction. Please accept the answer the first time!

Congratulations! You are all brilliant.

Genius is no longer for a select few. Each of you has been given special gifts, which are your geniuses. Realize what it is that you have been doing free all your life, but you do it so well that other people want to pay you to do it! Accept this as your genius. Then accept the fruits of your labor in the form of love, money, barter (whichever form of reward you desire).

Let us look at the process of taking THE TEST. Preparation to take the test starts the first day of class and you pick up the book and focus your mind on that subject. Scan in every books for each course. Open your mind to be curious. The next step is reading and mind mapping all your notes throughout the semester. The night before the test is another major part of the test taking adventure. It is important to go to bed at your usual time.   Place your glass of water by your bed.   Before you drift off to a peaceful sleep, scan in your mind-maps one more time.

The next morning, before you get out of bed, consciously breathe to your relaxed mind and then drink your water.   The water will trigger your reasoning mind to retrieve the information you stored in your relaxed mind. You will not need to write anything down.   This is a confidence builder. This process prepares you to recall all the information sitting in your long-term memory to respond to you during the test. There is no need to panic. All the information is there. All you have to do during the test is to breathe deeply relax, ask for the answer, and then record it. Enjoy all information running through your mind.

Next have a good breakfast.   Include your protein, which is food for the brain.   Then feed it fruit, which is energy for your brain. Stay away from pastry, caffeine and sugar. Drink juice, tea or water. Remember, the brain is the tool and the mind uses it to function.

This is one of the most important steps to taking the test: **BE ON TIME**! We have so many blocks of data registered in our reasoning mind on the fear of being late, and its repercussions.   Once you go into fear it takes time to breathe back to calm. Being late produces so much stress and fear that you may not be able to relieve yourself of the trauma before the test is over.   Fear of being late starts from the time we did not make it to the potty during our potty training. Then it progresses to elementary school when we were late to class, then to our jobs when we were late to work. So, do not even give those blocks of fear a chance to be activated before a test. Fear is the mind killer. Fear paralyzes your ability to think clearly.

While you are driving, riding or walking to this test taking adventure, continue to stay in your relaxed mind by consciously breathing in to the count of seven through your nose, hold for a count and then breathe out through your mouth to the count of 7. Stay relaxed! Stay focused! If other students are stressing, stay away from them. You have prepared well. There is no sense in joining them in their stress. You have been responsible and proactively sought knowledge for your higher use.

Get settled in your seat with whatever you need to take the test, such as sharpened No. 2 pencils. Continue to breathe and stay relaxed. Consciously breathe before you look at the test. Then scan the test all the way to the end that is allowed. If you are told not to go to the next page, just scan the one page. Then skim the entire test or the entire page. This gives your mind the opportunity to start retrieving the information you will need for each answer. Your mind will know which problem are the more complex and need more time. You are now ready to record your right answers.

Trust yourself! Trust Yourself! Trust Yourself!
You only know the RIGHT ANSWERS!

As you read the questions, immediately hear the right answer from your relaxed creative mind. If at any time you hear doubt, feel angry or fearful, just **STOP!** Consciously breathe to get back to your relaxed creative mind where your answers are waiting in your long-term memory. Then reread the question and **hear the right answer** in your mind. Record the right answer immediately without hesitation or identify the right answer if multiple choice.

Trust yourself. Hear the right answer and take the "A." The "A" belongs to you on your tests. You have earned the "A" by proactively preparing your mind to retrieve information from your long-term memory, reviewing this information and sleep incubating this information.

You must practice retrieving information from your relaxed mind all day long. The more you practice listening to your first response in your mind the better you will get at it. For 30 days I want you to practice listening to your first response and putting action behind those good thoughts.

We have thousands of thoughts in a day. Those thoughts bring you either peace or fear. If your thoughts put in you in fear, breathe to get to your relaxed creative mind then hear the opposite and equal peaceful thoughts. You are making choices all day long. Make it a peaceful choice.

Right Choices = *Right Learning*
Right Learning = *Right Answers*
Right Answers = *Inspired Life*

Congratulations on your choices!

SUMMARY
RELAXED RECALL
Test Taking Without Fear

This is your opportunity to allow the information you have stored in your long-term memory to flow from you with ease. There is no need for you to force the information out of you.

- You must just be open to receive the answer when you ask for it.
- You breathe into your long-term memory and scan in all the information
- You skim in the information
- You mind-map the information
- Review your mind-maps (notes) three to four times
- You incubate this information while you sleep peacefully in your relaxed creative mind where your long-term memory resides.

During this whole process, you were not guessing at answers, or recording misinformation or wrong information. Your mind only had the opportunity to learn and record the right answers. Your mind had the opportunity to condense and compress this information with everything that you have ever learned, so that you have full understanding of the total concept. There are no gaps of information missing in this process. Therefore:

You have learned one answer!
You have only stored the right answer!
You only know one answer!
You only know the right answer!

Believe in yourself and your own abilities!

Let us take a look at the process of taking THE TEST. Preparation to take the test starts the day you pick up the book, scanned in the entire book and focus your mind on that subject.

The night before the test:

❖ Go to bed at your usual time and place your glass of water by your bed. (Lie down and consciously breathe to your relaxed creative mind) before drifting off to a peaceful sleep, scan in your mind maps or notes. The morning of the test:

❖ Before getting out of bed, consciously breathe to your relaxed mind and drink your water;

❖ Have a good breakfast;

❖ While going to this test-taking adventure, continue to stay in your relaxed mind by consciously breath deeply.

❖ BE ON TIME!

• At the test:

❖ Get settled and consciously breathe deeply for 17 seconds.

❖ Scan, then skim as much of the test that is allowed:

❖ As you then read the questions, immediately hear the right answer from your relaxed mind;

❖ If you feel any doubt, anger, or fear, STOP and breathe consciously back to your relaxed mind, reread the question, and hear the right answer.

❖ Trust yourself! Hear the right answer and take the "A!"   ☙

©1993 Kadir Nelson

11
A Healthy Way to Learn

What you eat and drink while you are studying can greatly affect how well you learn and retain knowledge. The brain holds storage banks for your memory. If the brain gets sufficient nutritional food, energy, fluids and oxygen, then it can function efficiently for you to store your information. When you prepare to study, you must first prepare your mind to receive knowledge. You breathe deeply six times to open your mind to receive information and give information. But if you are tired and sluggish, your mind will also be tired and sluggish.

What you have put into the body will reflect many of your current life's circumstances. **Your food turns into your blood => your blood turns into your bodily fluids => your bodily fluids turn into your thoughts => your thoughts**

crystallize into your habits and your habits solidify into your life circumstances. So, your food begins the process. Fresh food has vibrant life and energy in it. Your human body still has life and energy in it. Therefore, it is important to add life and energy to your life and energy.

Please do not cook the life out of your vegetables. Raw or lightly steamed is great. The vibration quality of your food reflects the vibration quality of your physical condition. The condition of our physical body reflects the type of consciousness we are able to support. Please avoid overeating. Eat until comfortably satisfied.

Many people are dehydrated, mal-nourished and lack enough oxygen in their bodies. Your mind cannot perform for you efficiently under these conditions. When you first feel hungry, drink 8 oz. of water. Wait 20 minutes; if you are still hungry, please eat. Feed your brain with protein, and then energize your brain with natural sugars of fruits and vegetables. The brain is the tool that the mind uses.

Food for the Brain

It is important to eat protein, which is food for the brain. Excellent sources of protein are fish, poultry, fresh leafy greens, beans, peas, lentils and all kinds of nuts. Nuts, such as pecans, walnuts, cashews, almonds, filberts and peanuts are my favorite source of food for the brain.

Energy for the Brain

Once fed, then the brain needs energy. Fructose, the active sugar in fresh and dried fruits, fresh vegetables and juices, provide energy for the brain. I suggest the following fruits to eat while studying because they are easy to prepare and consume. Many of the fruits below can be eaten whole. Take great caution to rinse thoroughly.

Fresh Fruits

Apples	*Oranges*
Apricots	*Peaches*
Bananas	*Pears*
Blueberries	*Pineapple*
Cherries	*Plums*
Grapefruit	*Raspberries*
Grapes	*Strawberries*

I suggest the following fresh vegetables to eat while studying because they can be eaten alone, mixed, or with or without a dip or dressing. Preparation into bite size pieces is easy and they can be stored easily for continuous use. Again, take great caution to rinse thoroughly.

Fresh Vegetables

Broccoli	*Green Pepper*
Cauliflower	*Kale (YES Raw!)*
Carrots	*Lettuce (Leafy Green)*
Celery	*Spinach*
Cucumber	*Tomatoes*

Dried fruits and nuts can also provide an excellent source of energy for the brain. There is no preparation and can be kept in a jar on your desk or work area.

Dried Fruits and Nuts- Emily's Mixture

Pecans	Raisins
Walnuts	Dates
Cashews	Pineapple
Almonds	Papaya
Cranberries	Banana Chips
Cranberries	Cherries

Water for the Brain

Water is an essential element for the brain. Your brain and blood are composed of about four-fifths (4/5) water. Water makes up the principal part of the bodily fluids and regulates the body processes, especially the brain. Water is in every cell of your body. Water carries nutrients to your cells and waste matter from your body. Water acts as a natural lubricant to your limbs and joints, especially your spine. The more limber your spine, the better your health. Drink ½ your body weight measured in ounces of water per day to wash the inside of your body especially your brain. Adding a squeeze of lemon to your water is like adding detergent. Make water your favorite beverage and drink plenty while you are studying and during test taking. Water is "sky juice".

When you are studying, it is important to nourish the brain. The food that is eaten during the learning process becomes a cell that stores the information in your body for long term memory. Therefore, no breathing deeply, no water, no protein and no fructose results in no learning. Drinking water, eating smart, exercising, getting fresh air and sunshine, resting, relaxing and having fun combined with a peaceful environment, will contribute to your success during the learning process. ❧

EPILOGUE

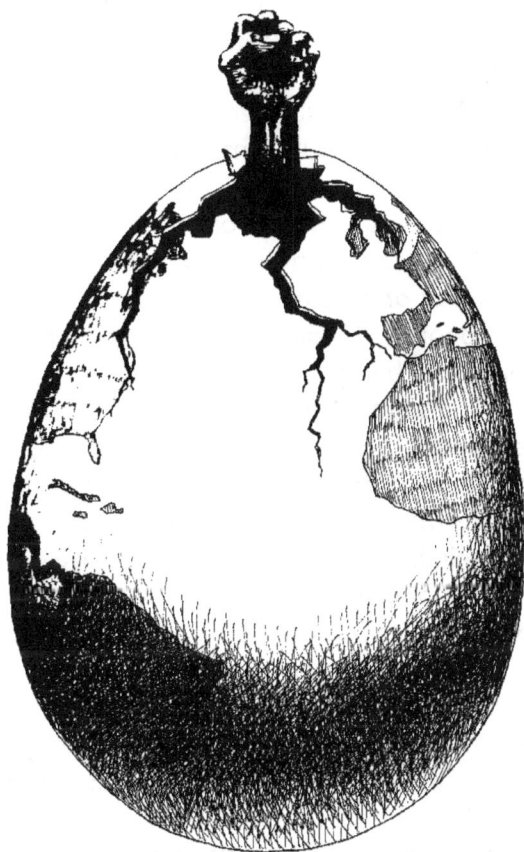

We learn something new every day because change is everywhere. Learning new information is a way of life. To resist change is to resist learning and living. To resist learning is to resist growing. When you stop growing you die mentally, emotionally and physically. When you stop growing, you become part of the world that is of the walking dead. Choose now to be of the walking, living, growing humankind on this planet. You now can learn anything you want. You can grow as long as you want. Choose now to enjoy change. Choose now to be a part of your life with compassion in Truth, Simplicity and Love.

When you stop growing, your mind will start to feed itself with what it already knows and whatever information it has available. This information can come from people you don't even like. This information can come from the television, newspaper or conversation you hear next to you by other people. Choose now to be in control of the information being stored in your mind.

The mind is like a muscle that must be exercised. You exercise your mind by using the Superlearning 3000 techniques in this book. Regular practice will strengthen your mind. By strengthening your mind, you will process massive information better and creative more ideas. You will accept change better because you are learning and understanding better, therefore, you will have less stress. Less stress will lead to fewer mistakes. Fewer mistakes will lead to more efficiency.

You are now prepared for the world we live in. Your once discouraged mind is now empowered to think freely and positively to come up with creative solutions to answer problems of all kinds. You now have better reasoning skills because you allow your relaxed creative mind to give your reasoning mind the whole concept for it to critically, logically and sequentially analyze. Your whole mind is working for you. Hearing the right answers, improves your self-confidence. You are now free from those limiting ideas about your own capabilities. Enjoy learning in this infinite field of all possibilities as you practice living in the Loving Nurturing Light of your Heart Space. Enjoy your peaceful journey to the 3rd Millennium.

Allow your life to flow! Allow your learning experience to flourish!
Enjoy your   journey.
Congratulations!

Practice what you have learned every day, even if only for 15 minutes.
Share with someone, what you have learned within 24 hours. This reinforces your learning and use.

Share with everyone that is around you all the time. This is your support base.
When you are not thinking well, those around you can remind you to center yourself by breathing.
Share your new knowledge with a friend!
Victory to New Knowledge!
Victory to New Creative Thoughts!
Victory to New Life of Learning!
ENJOY!!
Emily Diane Gunter

෴

References

Allen, James. As Man Thinketh. Marina Del Rey, CA: Devorss& Co.

Amen, Ra Un Nefer. 1990. Metu Neter, Vol. 1. Brooklyn, NY: Khamit Corporation.

Bach, Richard. 1973. Jonathan Livingston Seagull. New York: Avon Books.

Bolles, Richard N. 1972. What Color is Your Parachute? Berkeley, CA: Ten Speed.

Brown, G. Spencer. 1977. Laws of Form. New York: The Julian Press.

Brown, Les. 1972. Live Your Dreams. New York: Avon Books.

Buechner, Frederick. 1975. Wishful Thinking. New York: Harper Row.

Buzan, Tony, 1984, Make the Most of Your Mind. London, UK.

Chopra, Deepak. 1994. The Seven Laws of Success. San Rafael, CA: Amber-Allen Publ.

Delayne, Gayle. 1979. Living Your Dreams. New York: Harper Row.

Dick-Reed, Grantly. 1953. Childbirth Without Fear. New York: Harper Row.

Drummond, Henry. 1890. The Greatest Thing in the World. New York: J. Pott & Co.

Gardner, Howard. 1983. Frames of Mind. New York: Basic Books.

Gardner, Howard. 2000, Intelligence Reframed: Multiple Intelligences for the 21st Century.

Hill, Napoleon. 1972. Think and Grow Rich. New York: Hawthorn Books.

Houston, John P. 1981. Fundamentals of Learning and Memory. New York: Harcourt, Brace, Jovanovich, Inc.

Howard, Vernon. 1975. The Power of Your Supermind. Marina Del Rey, CA: DeVorss & Co.

Hutchinson, Michael. 1990. MegaBrain. New York: Ballantine Books.

Keyes, Ken Jr. 1978. Handbook to Higher Consciousness. KY: Living Love Publ.

Kloss, Jethro. 1975. <u>Back to Eden</u>. Santa Barbara, CA: Lifeline Books.

Loyd, Alex. 2010. <u>The Healing Code. New York, NY: Hachette</u>

Matz, Maxwell. 1969. <u>Psycho-Cybernetics</u>. New York: Pocket Books.

Mandino, Ob. 1972. <u>The Greatest Secret in the World</u>. New York: Pocket Books.

Ostrander, Sheila and Lynn Shroeder. 1979. <u>Superlearning</u>. New York: Dell Publ.

Peale, Norman Vincent. 1952. <u>Power of Positive Thinking</u>. New York: Fawcett Books. Papert, Seymour. 1980. <u>Mindstorm</u>. New York: Basic Books.

Prichard, Allyn. 1980. <u>Accelerated Learning</u>. Novato, CA: Academic Therapy Publication.

Redfield, James. 1993. Celestine <u>Prophecy</u>. New York: Warner Books.

Rose, Collin. 1994. <u>Accelerated Learning</u>. Great Britain.

Sinetar, Marsha. 1987. <u>Do What You Love and the Money will Follow</u>. New York: Dell Publ.

Three Initiates. 1912. <u>Kybalion</u>. Chicago: Yogi Publication Society.

Voss, Jeanette. 1991. <u>The Learning Revolution</u>, CA: Jalmar Press.

ABOUT THE AUTHOR EMILY DIANE GUNTER

Emily Diane Gunter is the Founder of the Rites of Passage Youth Empowerment Foundation dedicated to the cultural and educational empowerment for all people. Emily is also an inspirational motivational speaker whose message is mild but filled with a quality of love, beauty and strength. Emily is a keynote speaker, youth academic coach, retreat facilitator, seminar leader, educational consultant, spiritual life coach and author.

Emily traveled to Egypt where she lectured before representatives from seven Egyptian Universities. She has toured officiating over the Rites of Passage Youth Empowerment Retreats in the USA, France and UK. Emily also facilitates Elder Certification Retreats for communities interested in starting their own Rites of Passage Youth Empowerment Programs in schools, churches and community centers. Emily's new tour features the facilitation of The Seven Path Labyrinth for Playing and Learning Enhancements into the school teaching environment to enhance the academic and physical achievement potential. The foundation of all Emily's work is "The Power of Your Breath for Balance Lifelong Learning" since 1966 at American University.

Emily has trekked in the Himalayan Mountains of India, Tibet and Nepal while writing her books. She is the author of *Rites Of Passage to Spiritual Enlightenment-Living with Compassion.* Emily is also the author of *Superlearning 3000: learning made simple,* which promotes proactive learning through relaxed breathing and has 17 original illustrations from 1993 by Kadir Nelson. Emily's book, *"Thirteen Golden Keys to Learning: A Spiritual Journey"*, ©2005 is super learning with a touch of the spirit from within.

Emily taught Life and Learning Empowerments through relaxed breathing for 17,000 staff and clients of San Diego County Dept. of Social Work. She was a mathematics adjunct faculty member of Grossmont College when she was inspired to write her Superlearning book for her students who were failing math. Emily has been a consultant to the San Diego City Unified School District, City of Durham Human Resources and Park and Recreation, and the City of Rochester facilitating staff and youth development programs. Emily was the 2005 Keynote Speaker for the Defense Department Accounting Services/Air Force World Conference.

Emily received her Bachelor of Arts Degree in Mathematical Statistics from American University, Washington, D. C., in 1970 where she taught mathematics as an adjunct faculty member. Emily retired from Pacific Bell in San Diego in 1993 as a Telecommunications Engineer. Currently, she is the Director of Building Literacy through Arts and Culture for Urgent, Inc. in Miami, FL. Emily is listed in:

Who's Who in Mathematics and Science
Who's Who of Emerging Leader in America
Who's Who of America Women
Who's Who in Finance and Industry
Who's Who in the World

Contact Us:

Emily Diane Gunter
www.ritesofpassageonline.org
Saliha Nelson, Publisher
Urgent Press Publications
P. O. Box 013047
Miami, FL 33101
saliha@urgentinc.org

ALSO BY EMILY DIANE GUNTER

*Superlearning 2000: the New Technologies of Self-
Empowerment* ©1993
*Superlearning 2000: A Personal Handbook for the
Lifelong Learner* ©1995
*Superlearning 2000: Learning Made Simple-Everybody
Can Learn* ©1997
*A Rite of Passage to   Enlightenment: Living With
Compassion* ©2000
Rites of Passage Youth Empowerment Curriculum ©2002
Thirteen Golden Keys to Learning: A Spiritual Journey
©2005
Please visit the Urgent Press Publications website at:
Saliha Nelson at: **www.urgentinc.org**
Emily Diane Gunter at:
www.ritesofpassageonline.org
Kadir Nelson at**: www.kadirnelson.com**
Amin Nelson at: **www.littlebluerm.com**
Shedia Nelson at: **www.shedianelson.com**

www.ingramcontent.com/pod-product-compliance
Lightning Source LLC
Chambersburg PA
CBHW070815100426
42742CB00012B/2366